FUNDAMENTALS OF
FAST
❊ AND ❊
FRESH

(COOKING)

by SUSAN MITCHELL

ideals®

Ideals Publishing Corp.
Milwaukee, Wisconsin

C·O·N·T·E·N·T·S

ISBN 0-8249-3036-3
Copyright © MCMLXXXIV by Ideals Publishing Corp.
All rights reserved.
Printed and bound in the United States of America.

Published by Ideals Publishing Corporation
11315 Watertown Plank Road
Milwaukee, Wisconsin 53226
Published simultaneously in Canada

Photograph of Susan Mitchell by J. Edouard Ouellette,
Los Angeles, California

Introduction

The days pass hurriedly as we bustle from office desk to the nursery school, business meetings, whatever takes our time. Susan Mitchell understands our fast-paced lives that call for a hurry-up meal here, an eat-and-run meal there, and she appreciates our desire for delicious and healthy food. Susan doesn't just explain how to prepare quick meals, she also gives us recipes and meal planning ideas that encourage us to produce appetizing, health-enhancing meals.

Susan E. Mitchell's freelance career in food product, menu, and recipe development comes from the combination of fine training and practical experience in the world of cooking. Susan is a graduate of the London Cordon Bleu School of Cooking and holds a degree in home economics from Washington State University. She has worked as chef, manager, and consultant for restaurant chains and commercial food companies. She was instrumental in opening the first Good Earth restaurant.

Susan continues to serve as a food consultant and does food styling and product promotion for media tours. Her publications include articles for *Sunset Magazine*, *New Zealand Women's Weekly*, and restaurant trade journals. *Fundamentals of Fast and Fresh Cooking* is her third cookbook.

Susan's food philosophy is a blend of time-honored cooking techniques and the latest nutritional findings. Her presentation of simple cooking techniques includes principles by which basic recipes can be endlessly varied. Cooks are encouraged to go beyond Susan's own excellent recipes to create their own specialties.

Health-conscious cooks will appreciate the nutritional analyses that accompany the recipes. Calories, sodium, protein, and other nutritional elements in the recipes can be seen at a glance, enabling the cook to adapt her meal planning to accommodate any special requirements.

Take a few minutes to read about the basics of fast and fresh cooking and how you can use them every day in your own kitchen. And then, armed with Susan's cooking methods and philosophy, transform what might have been a humdrum meal into a special creation of your very own.

FAST AND FRESH
BASICS

Quick-Cooking Techniques

Professional chefs work efficiently because they understand and follow the principle of organized cooking. Every ingredient and utensil that will be needed is conveniently placed so that the work will flow smoothly. Hunting for mislaid utensils and missing ingredients is not only time-consuming but frustrating. So take some time to be certain that everything is *mise en place* — in its place — before you proceed with any recipe.

Another professional technique that eliminates work stoppages is that of pre-prepared or "pre-prepped" ingredients. You can make good use of this same strategy during weekends preparing for the week ahead.

Pre-preparation refers to long-term planning of menus, purchases, and storage. It especially involves measuring, chopping, and mixing of ingredients as far in advance of cooking as possible. With strategic pre-preparation, the cook can enter the kitchen and produce an excellent meal quickly and with little effort.

The Sauté

Menus from many luxury restaurants include sautéed fish, chicken, veal, or steak. Sautéing is a valuable cooking technique that enables a cook to complete entrees in just four to ten minutes. Finishing touches or quick sauces can be made ahead and added just before serving. Here are the basic instructions that will enable you to sauté any food perfectly.

Fish Fillets

The cooking time depends on the thickness and type of fish used. Melt 1 teaspoon butter (or clarified butter) and 1 teaspoon safflower or vegetable oil in a large skillet over medium-high heat. Place fillets, skin sides up, in the pan without crowding. When edges are opaque and curl slightly (about 1½ minutes for a thin sole fillet), flip the fillets over. Sauté 1½ minutes or until edges are opaque, golden, and fish flakes easily when tested in the thickest portion with a fork. Remove fillets to a serving dish. Serve with lemon wedges and a sprinkling of parsley, or a simple sauce.

Breast of Chicken, Veal Scallops, Veal Strips

Heat butter and oil as for fish fillets. Sauté (skin side up for chicken) without crowding for 3 minutes or until golden. Turn and sauté the other side for 3 to 5 minutes. Add butter or oil as needed. Finish chicken or veal as recipe indicates or improvise your own finishing touch.

Steak

Select boneless steak cuts about 1 inch thick. Allow ⅓ to ½ pound per person. Use tender cuts (rib, loin, or fillet). Heat oil and butter as for fish fillets. Sauté uncovered until well browned, about 3 to 5 minutes. Turn and sauté 3 to 5 minutes for rare to medium-rare.

The Fast Bake

This method cuts cooking time and gives food a crisp golden crust. Simply broil or bake the entree item in a 500° F. oven until golden. Then reduce heat to 350° F. Drain any accumulation of rendered fat. At this point, most meats require the addition of a braising broth to keep them from drying out.

Poaching Fish

Use two pounds of any fish fillets that are fairly thin. Fold skin side in, so that only the most attractive side is visible; place in a baking dish. If the fillets are thick, arrange, unfolded and overlapping, in the baking dish. Top with onion slices, if you like, and lemon. Pour on dry white wine to cover. Add a bouquet garni (bay leaf, pinch of thyme leaves, parsley sprig, carrot and celery stick, and 6 to 8 peppercorns), if desired. Bake at 400° for 15 to 20 minutes or until fillets flake easily when tested with a fork. Fillets should be opaque, white, and still moist.

While the fish is poaching, melt about 1 teaspoon butter over medium-high heat; drain cooking liquid into a measuring cup. Add water to equal 1 cup. Add this mixture to sautéed vegetables and cook, stirring constantly, until liquid is reduced and mixture thickens. Spoon sauce over fish. Top with shredded cheese or bread crumbs, if desired, and broil briefly until golden brown. Serve with a garnish of minced parsley and lemon slices or wedges.

Stir-Frying

Here's where organization, planning, and pre-prepping are a must!

Prepare vegetables to expose maximum surface area for cooking. Vegetables with thick stalks, such as broccoli and celery, should be cut in 1/8-inch diagonal slices. Cut mushrooms or cauliflowerets in 1/8-inch-thick straight slices. Green peppers or onions can be cut into strips or squares. Meat or poultry is usually cut in strips or 1-inch chunks.

To stir-fry, heat oil over high heat until it flows in small rivulets when the pan is tilted. Add onion and your choice of meat and brown lightly on both sides. Remove from pan. Heat a little more oil. Add root vegetables first. Add 1 tablespoon or more water as needed to cook vegetables tender-crisp without browning. Return meat and onion to pan along with desired cooking sauce. Stir constantly until thickened and clear.

Broiling

This is a speedy method of cooking the thicker cuts of meat or fish. For best results, the broiler must be hot enough (550° F.) to yield a browned exterior without overcooking the interior. Dry-fleshed fish or meat should be brushed with lemon juice or safflower oil before broiling to prevent drying out. Broil meat that is 1 inch thick about 4 inches from the heat source, turning once to brown both sides. Broil to desired doneness.

Weekly Menu Planning

Many of my students approach menu planning with a tentative attitude. They soon learn that a thirty-minute planning session and a single trip to the supermarket can organize the week's meals and simplify life immensely. Here's how to proceed.

Once a week, gather two sheets of paper, supermarket ads, *Fast and Fresh*, and your activity calendar. Label one sheet of paper "Grocery List" with subheadings for meat, dairy, produce, staples, and miscellaneous. Label the other sheet of paper "Master Menu Plan." Divide the menu plan into seven columns, one for each day of the week. Now, you're ready to plan, following these steps:

1. Check your calendar, noting on the menu plan those days that require an extra quick meal and any meals that will be eaten away from home.
2. Check ads for food sales and produce in season for lower prices.
3. Consider your own personal energy and cooking time needed and available for each day's meals.
4. Survey the refrigerator and freezer, noting which foods need to be used quickly. Also note staples that must be replenished and include them on your grocery list.
5. Now it's time to think of the fast and fresh meals you will enjoy preparing, giving thought to variety and personal favorites. List the entree first and then choose complementary side dishes, keeping in mind that you need a balance of food groups, color, texture, and flavors. Make your goal a menu mix of "pre-prepped" meals and fast dinners from scratch. Note where the recipes can be found and be sure that needed supplies are noted on the shopping list.

With this thirty-minute shopping plan you're ready to shop for the week. Head for the supermarket!

The Final Touch

The garnish adds a final touch that raises an otherwise ordinary dish to the level of edible art. In choosing the garnishes, think of the final plate presentation as an artistic composition. A different garnish for each dish will act as a highlight to catch the eye.

When choosing the garnish, remember that the goal is a contrast of colors and juxtaposition of textures.

Use any of the garnishes on the next page to add flair to any dish.

SALADS

Violets and nasturtium (whole flowers and leaves)

Herbs (fresh chopped leaves or whole sprigs)

Tomatoes (wedged or sliced, dipped in minced parsley or chives)

Eggs (hard-cooked, sliced, sieved, stuffed, or fluted)

Red and green peppers (cut in julienne strips)

Radishes (shredded or cut in julienne strips)

Pomegranite seed

Mushrooms (whole, sliced, or fluted)

Fennel (sliced)

Beets (cooked and cut into fancy shapes)

Cucumber slices (dipped in minced parsley)

Lemon wheels

Tomato roses

Pickles

Cherry tomatoes

Capers

Pearl onions

SOUPS

Snow peas

Vegetables (cut in julienne strips)

Egg noodles

Avocado chunks

Plain yogurt

Citrus slices

Sliced hard sausage

Toasted garlic croutons

Bean curd (tofu)

Sliced celery

Sliced parsley root

Croutons

Spaetzle

Small choux paste puffs (mini cream puffs)

Herb sprigs

Meat (cut in julienne strips)

Shredded cheese

Toasted rye sticks

ENTREES

Toasted nuts

Herb sprigs

Clusters of grapes

Citrus wheels (halved or twisted)

Citrus peel (grated)

Tomatoes (fluted, wedged, sliced, halved, whole)

Shredded cheese

Dairy products (plain yogurt, sour half-and-half, Neufchatel cheese)

Radishes (whole with stem, sliced, cut in julienne strips, or flowers)

Eggs (hard-cooked, sliced whites, sieved yolks)

Green onion (whole, cut in fans, minced)

Watercress or cilantro (bunches or sprigs)

Cucumbers (slices, twists)

Carrots (curls, sticks, rounds)

SIDE DISHES

Artichoke bottoms filled with tiny peas or vegetable slaws

Tomato halves fluted and filled with herbs and grated Parmesan cheese or vegetable puree

Red, yellow, and green peppers, tops removed, hollowed out and filled with sauces or dips

Cucumbers, ends cut off and hollowed out

Zucchini, cut in half lengthwise, scooped out and filled with vegetable puree

Onion or green pepper rings to hold bunches of asparagus

APPETIZERS

Spicy Clam Rounds

Makes 8 servings

⅓ cup small curd cottage cheese
Dash Worcestershire sauce
1 tablespoon Minceur Mayonnaise (recipe on page 42)
1 tablespoon lime juice
Pinch garlic powder

Dash hot pepper sauce
1 can (6½ ounces) minced clams, drained
Salt and freshly ground pepper to taste
Melba toast
Chopped parsley

In a blender or food processor, blend cottage cheese, Worcestershire sauce, mayonnaise, lime juice, garlic powder, and hot pepper sauce until smooth. Stir in clams, salt, and pepper. Just before serving, spread cheese mixture on melba toast; place on a small baking sheet. Broil about 4 inches from heat source until bubbly. Sprinkle with chopped parsley and serve at once.

NUTRITIONAL INFORMATION PER SERVING

Calories	52	Saturated Fat	0.3g	Fiber	0.05g	Potassium	39mg
Protein	5.1g	Cholesterol	4mg	Calcium	12mg	Sodium	83mg
Total Fat	1.7g	Carbohydrates	3.9g	Iron	0.2mg		

Anytime Barbecued Kebabs, 25

Dilled Cucumber Rounds

Makes 8 servings

1 cucumber
4 ounces Neufchatel cheese or kefir
1 tablespoon butter
Skim milk, heated
Salt and freshly ground pepper to taste

¼ cup chopped pimiento-stuffed olives
2 tablespoons minced parsley or green onions
½ teaspoon minced dillweed
Melba toast

Cut ends off cucumbers and core inside with a sharp knife or vegetable peeler. Stand on paper towels about 1 hour to drain. Pound the cheese and butter together, adding milk to thin, if necessary. Season with salt and pepper. Stir in olives, parsley, and dillweed. Using a pastry bag or small spoon, fill center of cucumber with cheese mixture. Wrap in plastic wrap and chill at least 30 minutes. Slice into thick rounds. Serve on melba toast.

NUTRITIONAL INFORMATION PER SERVING

Calories 73	Saturated Fat 3.0g	Fiber 0.13g	Potassium 70mg
Protein 2.2g	Cholesterol 15mg	Calcium 22mg	Sodium 196mg
Total Fat 5.4g	Carbohydrates 4.0g	Iron 0.2mg	

Dilled Shrimp

Makes 8 servings

Present this dip in an abalone or other scalloped sea shell and garnish with whole shrimp and fresh dillweed. The dip can also serve as a tasty sandwich spread. Try it as a topping for salad greens; garnish with sliced or slivered almonds.

½ cup Minceur Mayonnaise (recipe on page 42)
1 package (8 ounces) Neufchatel cheese, softened
4 ounces small shrimp, cooked and drained
1 teaspoon lemon juice

1 teaspoon Worcestershire sauce
2 tablespoons minced parsley
½ teaspoon minced garlic
¼ teaspoon minced dillweed

In a blender or food processor, combine mayonnaise and cheese. Stir in remaining ingredients. Cover and chill well before serving.

NUTRITIONAL INFORMATION PER SERVING

Calories 150	Saturated Fat 5.5g	Fiber 0.02g	Potassium 72mg
Protein 7.0g	Cholesterol 66mg	Calcium 47mg	Sodium 159mg
Total Fat 12.9g	Carbohydrates 1.9g	Iron 0.7mg	

Chile con Queso

Makes 10 servings

Traditionally, Chile con Queso requires a Mexican white cheese. This American version uses cream cheese.

1 tablespoon butter or margarine
1 medium onion, chopped
1 clove garlic, minced
1 can (8 ounces) stewed tomatoes
1 can (4 ounces) diced green chilies
½ teaspoon oregano leaves

¼ teaspoon salt
¼ teaspoon freshly ground pepper
1 package (8 ounces) Neufchatel cheese, cubed
4 to 5 tablespoons evaporated skim milk
Tortilla chips or crudités

In a skillet, melt butter. Sauté onion and garlic until tender. Stir in tomatoes, chilies, and seasonings. Simmer over medium heat, stirring often, for 10 minutes. Reduce heat; blend in cheese. Slowly stir in evaporated milk and heat through. Serve warm with tortilla chips or crudités.

NUTRITIONAL INFORMATION PER SERVING (includes 1 oz. chips per serving)

Calories 234	Saturated Fat 4.1g	Fiber 0.73g	Potassium 216mg
Protein 5.0g	Cholesterol 21mg	Calcium 75mg	Sodium 390mg
Total Fat 14.5g	Carbohydrates 16.5g	Iron 0.6mg	

Variation

• Substitute 1 pound grated Cheddar cheese for Neufchatel.

Tamale Appetizers

Makes 2 dozen

1 can (15 ounces) tamales
12 strips bacon, cut in halves
½ to 1 teaspoon chili powder

Pitted whole ripe olives
Mild or hot Mexican table sauce

Remove husks from tamales and cut into 1-inch lengths. Wrap each tamale piece in a piece of bacon and secure with a wooden pick. Sprinkle with chili powder. Place on a wire rack on a large baking sheet with sides. Broil about 10 minutes about 4 inches from heat source, turning once; or bake at 500° for 10 minutes. Press an olive onto each pick. Serve with Mexican table sauce.

NUTRITIONAL INFORMATION PER SERVING

Calories 63	Saturated Fat 0.43g	Fiber 0.32g	Potassium 11mg
Protein 1.7g	Cholesterol 2.7mg	Calcium 4.3mg	Sodium 246mg
Total Fat 4.9g	Carbohydrates 3.4g	Iron 0.3mg	

Prawns with Salsa Picante

Makes 10 servings

Any number of sauces are excellent with prawns. This one is easy — simply purchase a good quality Mexican table sauce and serve in a small crock. Style your sauce with additions of diced green or jalapeno chilies and garnish it with cilantro or parsley. The presentation is unique — a highly polished red apple holds the skewered prawns.

1 pound medium prawns or shrimp
(24 to 26 per pound)
1 to 1½ cups wine
Boiling water
1 clove garlic, minced

1 lemon, sliced
4 sprigs cilantro or parsley
Salt and freshly ground pepper to taste
Mexican table sauce

In a large saucepan, cover prawns with wine and enough boiling water to cover. Add garlic, lemon, cilantro, and salt and pepper. Cook over medium heat 3 to 5 minutes or until pink. Drain, cook, shell, and devein shrimp. Skewer shrimp with wooden picks. Spear the apple with the picks so that the shrimp are displayed in a fan-like arrangement. Serve with Mexican table sauce.

NUTRITIONAL INFORMATION PER SERVING

Calories	84	Saturated Fat	0.0g	Fiber	0.31g	Potassium	132mg
Protein	11.4g	Cholesterol	57mg	Calcium	63mg	Sodium	30mg
Total Fat	0.6g	Carbohydrates	4.1g	Iron	1.9mg		

Blue Cheese Dip

Makes 8 servings

1 package (8 ounces) Neufchatel cheese,
softened
¼ cup skim milk
1 tablespoon Minceur Mayonnaise
(recipe on page 42)

1 tablespoon dry vermouth
1 clove garlic, minced
¼ cup crumbled cheese, blue or Roquefort
2 tart apples, sliced

In a bowl, combine Neufchatel cheese, milk, mayonnaise, vermouth, and garlic; blend until smooth. Just before serving, stir in blue cheese. Serve with apple slices.

NUTRITIONAL INFORMATION PER SERVING

Calories	133	Saturated Fat	5.7g	Fiber	0.26g	Potassium	95mg
Protein	4.8g	Cholesterol	32mg	Calcium	81mg	Sodium	251mg
Total Fat	9.6g	Carbohydrates	7.7g	Iron	0.1mg		

Prawns with Salsa Picante, this page

Steamed Artichokes with Lemon or Dieters' Dip

Makes 6 servings

6 artichokes
3 lemons
¼ cup chopped fresh parsley

Freshly ground black pepper
Dieters' Dip

Trim tough bottom leaves off artichokes; cut off tips of remaining leaves with scissors; remove stems. Rub all exposed cut surfaces with a lemon cut in half to prevent their turning brown. Fill a large pot with water to a depth of 1 inch. Add juice of ½ lemon. Bring to a boil. Arrange artichokes in pot, stem side up. Place a wet towel over the top of the pot to prevent too much steam from escaping. Cook over medium heat until artichokes are tender, about 30 to 45 minutes. Serve with sliced lemon, parsley, and pepper; or with Dieters' Dip.

Dieters' Dip

½ cup each plain yogurt and Neufchatel cheese
¼ cup each grated celery and grated carrot

¼ teaspoon salt
¼ teaspoon dillweed

In a small bowl, combine ingredients. Chill. Serve with cold artichokes or asparagus.

NUTRITIONAL INFORMATION PER SERVING (INCLUDES ¼ CUP DIP)

Calories 103	Saturated Fat 3.2g	Fiber 2.97g	Potassium 494mg
Protein 6.3g	Cholesterol 17mg	Calcium 114mg	Sodium 220mg
Total Fat 5.3g	Carbohydrates 16.1g	Iron 1.6mg	

Southwestern Bean Dip

Makes 8 servings

This Tex-Mex dip is great served warm with corn or tortilla chips.

1 can (16 ounces) unseasoned or spicy
  refried beans
1 cup shredded sharp Cheddar cheese
¼ cup chopped green onions
¼ cup chopped parsley
  Chili powder to taste

2 to 3 tablespoons Mexican table or
  taco sauce
  Cherry tomato halves, minced parsley,
  or cilantro sprigs
  Corn or tortilla chips

In a saucepan or heatproof serving dish, combine refried beans, cheese, green onions, parsley, chili powder, and Mexican table sauce; blend well. Cook over medium heat, stirring constantly until well blended. Serve warm in a chafing dish or fondue pot. Garnish with cherry tomato halves, minced parsley, or cilantro sprigs. Serve with corn or tortilla chips.

NUTRITIONAL INFORMATION PER SERVING

Calories	132	Saturated Fat	3.2g	Fiber	0.90g	Potassium	248mg
Protein	7.8g	Cholesterol	17mg	Calcium	134mg	Sodium	114mg
Total Fat	5.8g	Carbohydrates	12.6g	Iron	1.6mg		

Variation

• Add one or more of the following to the prepared dip: green pepper, crumbled crisp-cooked bacon, garlic powder, or pepper.

Smoked Salmon Pâté

Makes 10 servings

This simply prepared, elegant pâté will add the crowning touch to any cocktail party.

2 packages (3 ounces each) smoked
  salmon, chopped
2 packages (8 ounces each) Neufchatel
  cheese
2 to 3 cloves garlic, minced

2 to 3 green onions, minced
1 to 2 tablespoons dry vermouth
  Caviar, watercress, minced green onion,
  and minced parsley

In a blender or food processor, blend salmon and cream cheese until smooth. Add garlic, green onions, and vermouth; blend well. Mound in a serving bowl; chill. Garnish with caviar, watercress, minced green onion, and parsley. Serve with vegetables or crackers.

NUTRITIONAL INFORMATION PER SERVING

Calories	163	Saturated Fat	7.2g	Fiber	0.04g	Potassium	71mg
Protein	9.0g	Cholesterol	45mg	Calcium	45mg	Sodium	240mg
Total Fat	12.5g	Carbohydrates	4.4g	Iron	0.4mg		

Eggplant Caviar

Makes 8 servings

*Also called "poor man's caviar," this excellent spread is not at all like real caviar.
Scoop it up with romaine leaves, pita bread, or Armenian crackers.*

1 large eggplant, sliced lengthwise in half
2 tablespoons red or white wine vinegar
1 tablespoon lemon juice
1 teaspoon olive oil
¼ teaspooon ground cumin
¼ teaspoon cinnamon
⅛ teaspoon allspice

Salt and pepper to taste
3 tablespoons minced parsley
1 clove garlic, minced
2 tomatoes, chopped
2 green onions, chopped
Cilantro or parsley sprigs

Place eggplant in a shallow baking dish or on a baking sheet. Bake at 375° F. for 30 minutes or until softened. In a bowl, combine vinegar, lemon juice, oil, spices, parsley, and garlic; blend well. Add salt and pepper, if desired. Dip eggplant in cold water, peel off skin, and dice pulp. Combine diced eggplant, tomatoes, and green onions. Pour dressing over vegetable mixture. Cover and chill well before serving. Garnish with cilantro.

NUTRITIONAL INFORMATION PER SERVING

Calories	28	Saturated Fat	0.1g	Fiber	0.35g	Potassium	210mg
Protein	1.2g	Cholesterol	0mg	Calcium	25mg	Sodium	38mg
Total Fat	0.8g	Carbohydrates	8.1g	Iron	0.9mg		

Great Guacamole

Makes 6 servings

*This is one of many variations, so feel free to experiment with your own. To prevent
discoloration, stir a little mayonnaise and citrus juice into dip.*

2 large ripe avocados
2 to 3 tablespoons lemon or lime juice
1 tablespoon finely chopped onion
1 clove garlic, minced
½ can (4 ounces) California green chilies, diced

6 tablespoons Mexican salsa; salt and pepper
  to taste
1 small tomato, chopped
3 tablespoons black and red caviar or twisted
  lemon slices, cherry tomatoes, and cilantro

In a small bowl, blend all ingredients except tomato. Fold in tomato. Garnish with red and black caviar, or lemon slices, cherry tomatoes, and cilantro. Serve with raw vegetables.

NUTRITIONAL INFORMATION PER SERVING (INCLUDES CAVIAR)

Calories	179	Saturated Fat	2.1g	Fiber	2.47g	Potassium	626mg
Protein	4.5g	Cholesterol	0mg	Calcium	42mg	Sodium	231mg
Total Fat	14.8g	Carbohydrates	11.9g	Iron	2.2mg		

Southwestern Bean Dip, 17; Eggplant Caviar, this page

Filled Puffs

Makes 10 puffs

Pastry Puffs

1 cup water
½ cup butter
⅛ teaspoon salt

1⅛ cups sifted flour
4 eggs
Clam Filling

Preheat oven to 425° F. In a heavy saucepan, bring water, butter, and salt to a boil; remove from heat. Add flour all at once; return to heat. Stir vigorously until mixture forms a ball and pulls away from sides of pan. Transfer to a mixing bowl or food processor. Add eggs, 1 at a time, beating well after each addition. Beat until dough is thick and shiny. Use 2 spoons or a pastry bag fitted with a ½-inch tip to drop 1-inch mounds about 2 inches apart onto an ungreased baking sheet. Bake at 425° F. for about 15 minutes or until crisp and golden brown. Cool completely before storing. Cut each puff horizontally almost in half. Stuff each puff with Clam Filling.

Clam Filling

3 cans (7 ounces each) minced clams, drained
2 packages (8 ounces each) Neufchatel
    cheese, softened
2 tablespoons minced green onion

2 tablespoons minced celery
½ teaspoon Worcestershire sauce
Dash hot pepper sauce
Salt and freshly ground pepper to taste

In a small bowl, combine all ingredients; blend well.

NUTRITIONAL INFORMATION PER SERVING

Calories 330	Saturated Fat 13.1g	Fiber 0.06g	Potassium 106mg
Protein 15.3g	Cholesterol 170mg	Calcium 52mg	Sodium 360mg
Total Fat 23.2g	Carbohydrates 14.3g	Iron 0.9mg	

Variations

- **Clam Pastry Puffs**   Reserve clam juice from the 3 cans minced clams used in Clam Filling. Add water to equal 1 cup. Substitute this 1 cup clam liquid mixture for the 1 cup water in the Pastry Puff recipe.

- **Crab Filled Puffs**   Substitute shredded crab meat for the clams and season with dillweed to taste.

- **Cheese Filled Puffs**   Stuff baked and cooled puffs with cubes of cheese. Heat in oven until cheese is soft. Serve at once.

Golden Puffs

Makes 30 puffs

This recipe can be made in advance, frozen, and reheated before serving.

1 cup water
¼ cup butter
⅛ teaspoon salt
1¼ cups all-purpose flour

3 eggs
¾ cup shredded Gruyere or Swiss cheese
¼ teaspoon cayenne pepper
¼ teaspoon dry mustard

Preheat oven to 425° F. In a heavy saucepan, bring water, butter, and salt to a boil; remove from heat. Add flour all at once; return to heat. Stir vigorously until mixture forms a ball and pulls away from sides of pan. Remove from heat. Add eggs, 1 at a time, beating well after each addition. Beat until smooth and shiny. Add cheese, cayenne, and mustard; blend well. Use 2 spoons or a pastry tube fitted with a ½-inch tip to drop 1-inch mounds about 2 inches apart onto a large baking sheet. Bake for 10 minutes or until golden brown. Serve at once.

NUTRITIONAL INFORMATION PER PUFF

Calories 54	Saturated Fat 1.7g	Fiber 0.01g	Potassium 15mg
Protein 2.1g	Cholesterol 35mg	Calcium 33mg	Sodium 56mg
Total Fat 3.1g	Carbohydrates 4.4g	Iron 0.3mg	

Steak Tartare

Makes 6 servings

1½ pounds very lean ground sirloin
   or top round
2 shallots or green onions, minced
2 anchovy fillets, mashed
1 tablespoon red wine vinegar
2 teaspoons soy sauce
2 teaspoons Dijon-style mustard
2 teaspoons brandy

2 cloves garlic, minced
1 tablespoon minced parsley
1 teaspoon salt
Freshly ground pepper to taste
Watercress
Gherkins or cornichons, chopped shallots,
capers, anchovies, chopped hard-cooked
egg whites, cherry tomatoes

Combine ground sirloin, shallots, anchovies, vinegar, soy sauce, mustard, brandy, garlic, parsley, salt, and pepper; blend well. Shape mixture into a ball. Line a serving platter with watercress. Place steak tartare in center. Press an egg shell into the top of the ball of steak. Place raw egg yolk inside the shell as a garnish. Arrange gherkins and other garnishes around edge of platter.

NUTRITIONAL INFORMATION PER SERVING

Calories 257	Saturated Fat 5.2g	Fiber 0.04g	Potassium 180mg
Protein 35.4g	Cholesterol 79mg	Calcium 15mg	Sodium 527mg
Total Fat 11.0g	Carbohydrates 3.8g	Iron 1.8mg	

Herb Cheese Mold

Makes 6 servings

Make a Boursin or Rondele cheese by experimenting with as many as four different herbs, minced garlic, parsley, and lemon juice.

1 package (8 ounces) Neufchatel cheese, softened
2 to 3 tablespoons lemon juice
½ teaspoon freshly ground pepper

2 tablespoons minced parsley
1 clove garlic, minced
¼ teaspoon each of 4 herbs of your choice
Skim milk

In a small mixing bowl, combine cheese, lemon juice, pepper, parsley, and garlic. Add herbs, tasting mixture with each addition. Beat cheese mixture until smooth, adding milk to thin, if necessary. Mound in a small serving bowl, press into a greased mold, or shape otherwise as desired. Cover and chill well before serving.

NUTRITIONAL INFORMATION PER SERVING

Calories 105	Saturated Fat 5.6g	Fiber 0.09g	Potassium 78mg
Protein 4.0g	Cholesterol 29mg	Calcium 40mg	Sodium 154mg
Total Fat 8.8g	Carbohydrates 3.8g	Iron 0.2mg	

Variations

- Garnish with toasted pine nuts or slivered almonds arranged like porcupine quills.
- Shape cheese mixture into a ball and roll in parsley or paprika.

Orange Curry Tea

Makes 4 servings

This is an aromatic beverage that is wonderful to begin or end your party.

1 teaspoon butter
4 to 5 whole cloves
1 stick cinnamon, broken in half
¼ teaspoon each cumin seed and mustard seed

Dash cayenne
1 teaspoon freshly grated ginger
Cardamom seeds from 2 pods
1 quart orange juice

In a large saucepan, heat butter with spices. Add orange juice and heat on low heat for 15 minutes. Serve hot in small bowls or cups.

NUTRITIONAL INFORMATION PER SERVING

Calories 124	Saturated Fat 0.6g	Fiber 0.36g	Potassium 511mg
Protein 1.8g	Cholesterol 3mg	Calcium 33mg	Sodium 13mg
Total Fat 1.6g	Carbohydrates 26.4g	Iron 0.7mg	

Herb Cheese Molds, this page; Filled Puffs, 20

Cheese Fondue

Makes 6 servings

8 ounces Swiss cheese, grated
8 ounces Gruyere cheese, grated
3 tablespoons flour
  Dash nutmeg
  Dash dry mustard
1 to 2 cloves garlic, halved
1½ cups dry white wine, such as Swiss Fondant
  or Johannesberg Riseling

Freshly ground black pepper
2 to 4 tablespoons kirsch, brandy or Cognac
  Cubed French sourdough or Italian bread
  Cooked hot or mild Italian sausage,
  cut in bite-size pieces
  Sliced salami

In a bowl, toss cheese with flour, nutmeg, and dry mustard. Rub inside of fondue pot with cut sides of garlic. Heat fondue pot and pour in wine. When wine begins to bubble, turn the heat down and begin adding cheese mixture, a small amount at a time, stirring with a wooden spoon. Grind in pepper to taste; add kirsch to taste. Serve immediately with bread, sausage, and salami. Do not let fondue come to a boil.

NUTRITIONAL INFORMATION PER SERVING

Calories 391	Saturated Fat 13.9g	Fiber 0.05g	Potassium 132mg
Protein 22.7g	Cholesterol 76mg	Calcium 758mg	Sodium 231mg
Total Fat 22.9g	Carbohydrates 10.9g	Iron 0.6mg	

Variations

- **Mexican** Substitute mild Cheddar for Gruyere and 2 to 4 tablespoons Mexican table sauce for liqueur. Add 1 can (4 ounces) diced green chilies.
- **Vegetarian** Instead of serving with sausage and salami, serve with quartered and cooked new potatoes, artichoke hearts, green pepper squares, broccoli flowerets, or cauliflowerets.

Anytime Barbecued Kebabs

Makes 6 servings

Use your imagination and design your own kebabs! Skewer a selection of meat, poultry, fish, and vegetables. Marinate, if desired; grill or broil. Serve with a choice of sauces.

Vegetables and Fruit

1 large onion, cut in chunks
1 large green pepper or red pepper,
   cut in squares
10 to 12 large mushrooms
8 to 10 cherry tomatoes
6 to 8 ears frozen baby corn
8 to 10 cubes eggplant or zucchini
   or crookneck squash
8 small white onions
8 pineapple chunks

Meat, Poultry, and Fish

2 pounds cubed lamb (leg or shoulder
roast), or cubed beef top round,
or chicken or turkey breast
1½ pounds medium prawns or shrimp
1½ pounds thick fish fillets,
   cut into chunks

Marinades

Mediterranean
   Marinade
Indian Yogurt
   Marinade

Sauces

Sweet and Sour
Sauce

Mediterranean Marinade

¼ cup olive oil
¼ cup lemon juice
¼ cup water
2 to 3 cloves garlic, minced

1 teaspoon basil leaves
½ teaspoon salt
¼ teaspoon ground coriander
¼ teaspoon freshly ground pepper

Blend all ingredients. Pour marinade over prepared kebabs. Marinate for 1 hour 30 minutes, turning once. Drain marinade from kebabs. Grill as desired.

Indian Yogurt Marinade

1 cup plain yogurt
1 small red onion, chopped
2 cloves garlic, minced
1 tablespoon minced crystallized ginger
1½ teaspoons ground cumin
1 teaspoon nutmeg

1 teaspoon chili powder
½ teaspoon cinnamon
½ teaspoon freshly ground pepper
¼ teaspoon ground cloves
¼ teaspoon ground cardamom

Combine all ingredients. Marinate as for Mediterranean Marinade.

Sweet and Sour Sauce

8 ounces fresh or canned pineapple,
   puréed
1 tablespoon soy sauce
1 tablespoon brown sugar
1 tablespoon vinegar

1 to 2 cloves garlic, minced or pressed
¼ teaspoon ground ginger
1 tablespoon cornstarch
1 tablespoon water

In a small saucepan, combine pineapple puree, soy sauce, brown sugar, vinegar, garlic, and ginger. Bring to a boil; reduce heat. Simmer for 10 minutes. Dissolve cornstarch in water. Stir into sauce. Cook, stirring constantly, until sauce thickens.

SOUPS

Quick Minestrone

Makes 4 servings

 1 teaspoon olive oil
⅓ cup chopped cooked ham
⅓ cup chopped onion
⅓ cup sliced celery
 1 to 2 cloves garlic, minced
 4 cups Chicken Broth (recipe on page 121)
 3 tomatoes, diced, or 1 can (16 ounces)
   tomatoes with liquid, broken up

 2 small zucchini squash, sliced
 1 large carrot, sliced
 1 cup chopped or shredded Savoy cabbage
 1 can (16 ounces) garbanzo beans, drained
 ½ teaspoon rosemary or sage leaves
 ½ cup elbow macaroni
   Grated Parmesan cheese

In a 6-quart kettle, heat oil. Sauté ham, onion, celery, and garlic until vegetables are tender. Add broth, tomatoes, zucchini, carrot, cabbage, garbanzo beans, and rosemary. Bring to a boil; reduce heat. Simmer 20 minutes. Add macaroni; simmer 10 minutes. Garnish each serving with Parmesan cheese.

NUTRITIONAL INFORMATION PER SERVING

Calories 293	Saturated Fat 0.8g	Fiber 3.74g	Potassium 1118mg
Protein 19.3g	Cholesterol 1mg	Calcium 135mg	Sodium 335mg
Total Fat 5.8g	Carbohydrates 45.5g	Iron 5.0mg	

Quick Minestrone, this page
Overleaf; Cream-of-Anything Soup, 30

Cream-of-Anything Soup

Makes 5 servings

This soup is low in the 3 C's — calories, cost, and cholesterol. There are endless possibilities for varying and combining pureed vegetables. Thin this soup for sipping, and try it both hot and cold.

1 tablespoon butter
1 medium red or yellow onion, or
  1 bunch green onions, minced
1 tablespoon flour
¼ cup nonfat dry milk
1 can (13 ounces) evaporated skim milk
2 cups Chicken Broth (recipe on page 121) or
  canned unsalted broth

1 pound vegetables, your choice: carrots or
  celery, finely chopped; broccoli or
  cauliflower, broken into flowerets; 1 pound
  mushrooms, coarsely chopped; 2 bunches
  spinach or watercress; 1 bunch chard, kale,
  or sorrel
4 cups shredded lettuce
Salt and white pepper

In a large saucepan, melt butter. Sauté onion over medium heat about 3 minutes or until tender. Stir in flour and dry milk; cook until bubbly, stirring constantly. Gradually add evaporated milk, stirring until smooth. Add chicken broth. Add long-cooking or root vegetables and bring to a boil; reduce heat. Simmer, stirring occasionally, until soup thickens and vegetables are tender-crisp. Add leafy vegetables. Cover and cook 3 minutes or until wilted. Add salt and pepper. In a blender or food processor, blend soup in batches until smooth. Serve hot or chilled.

――――――――――――――――――**Variations**――――――――――――――――――

- **Cream of Carrot Soup**   Add ½ to 1 teaspoon chopped dillweed, tarragon, or thyme. Garnish each serving with a lemon slice and a dollop of plain yogurt.
- **Cream of Broccoli Soup**   Top each serving with ½ cup shredded sharp Cheddar cheese.
- **Cream of Mushroom Soup**   Omit broth. Add one cup plain yogurt and 1 additional can evaporated skim milk. Stir in ¼ cup minced parsley. Add a dash of mace or nutmeg. Garnish with sour half-and-half or kefir.
- **Cream of Watercress Soup**   Garnish with a lemon slice and sprigs of watercress.
- **Cream of Spinach Soup**   Add ¼ teaspoon thyme or marjoram leaves. Garnish with a sprinkling of sieved egg yolk.
- **Cream of Lettuce Soup**   Add dry sherry to taste and a dash of paprika or nutmeg.

Seafood Bisque

Makes 4 servings

Vary the seafood as your budget and preference dictate.

2 tablespoons butter
2 tablespoons chopped onion
2 tablespoons flour
1 cup skim milk, heated
¾ to 1 pound cooked shrimp or 1 to 1½ pints oysters with liquid (or combination)

1 can (3½ ounces) crab meat, drained and flaked
½ cup evaporated skim milk
3 tablespoons dry sherry
2 tablespoons chopped parsley or chives
Salt, paprika, and nutmeg to taste

In a large saucepan, melt butter. Sauté onion until golden. Add flour; cook until bubbly, stirring constantly. Gradually add skim milk; stir constantly until the mixture thickens and bubbles. Add shrimp, crab meat, and evaporated skim milk. Heat through but do not boil. Stir in sherry, parsley, salt, paprika, and nutmeg.

NUTRITIONAL INFORMATION PER SERVING

Calories 268	Saturated Fat 3.7g	Fiber 0.13g	Potassium 373mg
Protein 33.4g	Cholesterol 174mg	Calcium 303mg	Sodium 196mg
Total Fat 7.7g	Carbohydrates 11.8g	Iron 3.9mg	

Cool Cucumber Soup

Makes 4 servings

2 cucumbers, peeled, seeded, and cut in julienne strips
2 slices onion
½ bay leaf, optional
1 can (13 ounces) evaporated skim milk
2 sprigs parsley

2 tablespoons flour
½ cup Chicken Broth (recipe on page 121) or canned unsalted broth
½ cup Sauterne or Bordeaux wine
Salt and freshly ground white pepper

In a large saucepan, combine cucumbers, onion, bay leaf, evaporated milk, and parsley. Simmer about 10 minutes or until vegetables are tender. In a small saucepan, blend flour into chicken broth to make a paste; cook until bubbly, stirring constantly. Blend broth mixture into hot vegetable mixture; stir until thickened. In a blender or food processor, blend soup in batches until smooth. Stir in wine, salt, and pepper. Refrigerate until well chilled. Garnish as desired.

NUTRITIONAL INFORMATION PER SERVING

Calories 139	Saturated Fat 0.1g	Fiber 0.32g	Potassium 539mg
Protein 9.6g	Cholesterol 4mg	Calcium 323mg	Sodium 204mg
Total Fat 0.4g	Carbohydrates 19.4g	Iron 1.0mg	

Chilled Crookneck Soup

Makes 6 servings

This chilled soup has a kick of cumin and a sunny, golden color.

4 crookneck squash, sliced
1 medium carrot, sliced
1 large red onion, chopped
1 leek, white part only, chopped
2 to 3 cloves garlic, minced
¼ to ½ teaspoon ground cumin

¼ teaspoon nutmeg
3 cups Chicken Broth (recipe on page 121)
    Cayenne pepper to taste
¼ cup plain yogurt
¼ cup chopped chives

In a large saucepan, combine first 8 ingredients. Bring to a boil; reduce heat. Cover and simmer for 15 minutes or until vegetables are tender. Add cayenne. In a blender or food processor, blend soup in batches until smooth. Refrigerate until chilled. Garnish each serving with 1 tablespoon each of yogurt and chives. If a thinner soup is desired, stir in more chicken broth until soup is of desired consistency.

NUTRITIONAL INFORMATION PER SERVING

Calories	70	Saturated Fat	0.4g	Fiber	1.37g	Potassium	439mg
Protein	5.0g	Cholesterol	2mg	Calcium	73mg	Sodium	54mg
Total Fat	1.3g	Carbohydrates	13.9g	Iron	1.5mg		

Clam and Mushroom Bisque

Makes 4 servings

1 tablespoon butter
½ pound mushrooms, chopped
2 tablespoons flour
2 cans (10 ounces each) minced
    clams and liquid

2 cups clam broth
1 cup evaporated skim milk
½ teaspoon thyme leaves
    Salt and freshly ground pepper to taste
    Chopped parsley or chives

In a large saucepan, melt butter. Sauté mushrooms about 3 minutes or until just tender. Add flour; cook until bubbly, stirring constantly. Add clams and broth; simmer 5 minutes. Stir in milk. Heat through but do not boil. Season with thyme, salt, and pepper. Garnish each serving with parsley.

NUTRITIONAL INFORMATION PER SERVING

Calories	209	Saturated Fat	1.8g	Fiber	0.57g	Potassium	483mg
Protein	23.0g	Cholesterol	10mg	Calcium	202mg	Sodium	180mg
Total Fat	5.8g	Carbohydrates	15.4g	Iron	1.2mg		

Mushroom and Brown Rice Soup

Makes 8 servings

Experiment with a variety of mushrooms: wild, domestic, or imported.

1 pound mushrooms
1 teaspoon butter
1 large red onion, chopped
2 quarts Chicken Broth (recipe on page 121)
1 to 1½ cups brown rice (or combination brown and wild rice) or pearl barley

1 bay leaf
Salt and freshly ground pepper to taste
Watercress sprigs
Plain yogurt or Neufchatel cheese

Slice mushroom caps; chop mushroom stems. In a 6-quart kettle, melt butter. Sauté mushrooms and onion over medium heat for 6 to 8 minutes or until tender. Add broth, rice, and bay leaf. Bring to a boil; reduce heat. Cover and simmer for 30 minutes. Remove bay leaf. Season with salt and pepper. Garnish with watercress sprigs and dollops of yogurt.

NUTRITIONAL INFORMATION PER SERVING

Calories 109	Saturated Fat 0.9g	Fiber 0.74g	Potassium 521mg
Protein 7.9g	Cholesterol 3mg	Calcium 39mg	Sodium 133mg
Total Fat 2.6g	Carbohydrates 13.4g	Iron 1.3mg	

Cream of Lentil Soup

Makes 4 servings

1 cup lentils
5 cups water
¼ bay leaf
2 tablespoons diced onion

1 tablespoon butter
Salt to taste
Crumbled mint

Wash lentils with cold water. In a large saucepan, bring water to a boil. Add lentils and bay leaf; simmer 45 minutes. In a small saucepan, melt butter. Sauté onion until tender. Add to partially drained lentils and mash, sieve, or puree the entire mixture. Season to taste. Add a bit of crumbled mint to each bowl of soup, if desired.

NUTRITIONAL INFORMATION PER SERVING

Calories 189	Saturated Fat 1.8g	Fiber 1.95g	Potassium 385mg
Protein 11.8g	Cholesterol 8mg	Calcium 40mg	Sodium 111mg
Total Fat 3.4g	Carbohydrates 2.9g	Iron 3.3mg	

Wild Rice and Cheese Soup

Makes 12 servings

¼ cup butter
1 large red onion, finely chopped
2 ribs celery, thinly sliced
¼ to ½ pound mushrooms, chopped
1 to 2 carrots, grated
½ cup flour
8 cups Chicken Broth (recipe on page 121)

1 cup evaporated skim milk
2 cups cooked wild rice
2 cups shredded sharp or mild Cheddar cheese
2 to 3 tablespoons dry white wine
   Shredded Cheddar cheese, minced onion,
   or parsley

In a 6-quart kettle, melt butter. Sauté onion, celery, mushrooms, and carrots for 3 to 5 minutes or until vegetables are tender-crisp. Stir in flour; cook until bubbly but not browned, stirring constantly. Gradually stir in broth and milk; blend until smooth. Bring to a boil; reduce heat. Simmer for 15 minutes. Stir in rice, cheese, and wine. Heat through but do not boil. Garnish with additional shredded cheese, minced onion, or parsley.

NUTRITIONAL INFORMATION PER SERVING

Calories 207	Saturated Fat 6.1g	Fiber 0.41g	Potassium 363mg
Protein 11.8g	Cholesterol 31mg	Calcium 227mg	Sodium 265mg
Total Fat 11.2g	Carbohydrates 14.1g	Iron 1.2mg	

Delicate Green Pea Soup

Makes 4 servings

1 teaspoon butter
1 medium onion, sliced
1 medium carrot, grated
2 cups Chicken Broth (recipe on page 121)
1 package (10 ounces) frozen early peas,
   thawed

1 teaspoon chervil leaves
¼ cup white wine
¼ cup evaporated skim milk
   Mint leaves or plain yogurt

In a large saucepan, melt butter. Sauté onion and carrot until tender. Add remaining ingredients and heat through. In a blender or food processor, blend soup in batches until smooth. Refrigerate until chilled. Garnish with mint leaves or a dollop of yogurt.

NUTRITIONAL INFORMATION PER SERVING

Calories 133	Saturated Fat 1.2g	Fiber 1.77g	Potassium 371mg
Protein 8.5g	Cholesterol 6mg	Calcium 100mg	Sodium 153mg
Total Fat 2.6g	Carbohydrates 16.7g	Iron 1.7mg	

Delicate Green Pea Soup, this page

Saffron Pumpkin Soup

Makes 6 servings

For an eye-catching presentation, serve this beautiful golden soup in the pumpkin shell.

½ cup sliced green onions
1 small red onion, minced
1½ cups Vegetable Broth (recipe on page 114)
4 cups seeded and coarsely chopped
    cooking pumpkin

1 bay leaf
    Pinch saffron powder
¼ teaspoon freshly ground white pepper
½ cup skim milk, scalded

In a large saucepan, cook the onions in the vegetable broth until tender. Stir in the pumpkin, bay leaf, saffron, and white pepper. Cover and simmer for 30 minutes. Discard bay leaf. In a blender or food processor, blend soup in batches until smooth. Stir in skim milk. Serve at once.

NUTRITIONAL INFORMATION PER SERVING

Calories 74	Saturated Fat 0.0g	Fiber 2.28g	Potassium 465mg
Protein 3.0g	Cholesterol 0mg	Calcium 75mg	Sodium 16mg
Total Fat 0.7g	Carbohydrates 16.5g	Iron 0.9mg	

Vichyssoise

Makes 10 servings

1 teaspoon butter
3 or 4 leeks, cut in ½-inch slices, using
    the white part and half of the green tops
1 medium onion, diced
4 potatoes, peeled and diced

4 cups Chicken Broth (recipe on page 121)
1 can (13 ounces) evaporated skim milk
1 carton (8 ounces) plain yogurt
¼ to ⅓ cup minced chives
    Salt and freshly ground pepper to taste

In a large saucepan, melt butter. Add leeks and onion. Cover and cook until vegetables are tender, stirring occasionally. Add potatoes and broth. Cover and simmer for 15 minutes. In a blender or food processor, blend soup in batches until smooth. Return to saucepan. Blend in milk and yogurt. Heat through but do not boil. Season with salt and pepper. Garnish each serving with chives.

NUTRITIONAL INFORMATION PER SERVING

Calories 155	Saturated Fat 1.0g	Fiber 1.11g	Potassium 702mg
Protein 8.9g	Cholesterol 6mg	Calcium 186mg	Sodium 126mg
Total Fat 2.0g	Carbohydrates 25.7g	Iron 1.4mg	

Vegetable Barley Soup

Makes 8 servings

Go ahead and double the recipe, it's so good and warming.
The yogurt gives it unusual style.

6 to 8 black peppercorns
1 bay leaf
4 sprigs parsley
1 teaspoon thyme leaves
1 tablespoon safflower oil
3 medium carrots, peeled and sliced
2 ribs celery, sliced
1 large red onion, sliced

½ pound green beans, diagonally sliced
1 turnip or parsnip, diced
2 to 3 cloves garlic, minced or pressed
2 tablespoons tomato paste
1 cup barley
5 cups Vegetable Broth (recipe on page 114)
1 cup plain yogurt
Salt and freshly ground pepper to taste

Make a bouquet garni of first 4 ingredients; set aside. In a large saucepan, heat oil. Sauté carrots, celery, onion, green beans, turnip, and garlic about 5 minutes or until vegetables are tender. Stir in tomato paste. Add barley, broth, and bouquet garni; simmer for 20 minutes or until vegetables and barley are tender. Discard bouquet garni. In a blender or food processor, blend soup in batches until smooth. Blend in yogurt. Return to saucepan. Heat through but do not boil. Season with salt and pepper.

NUTRITIONAL INFORMATION PER SERVING

Calories 169	Saturated Fat 0.8g	Fiber 1.30g	Potassium 358mg
Protein 5.6g	Cholesterol 4mg	Calcium 94mg	Sodium 81mg
Total Fat 3.6g	Carbohydrates 33.8g	Iron 1.9mg	

SALADS

Mexican Taco Salad

Makes 4 servings

Beef, ham, tongue, or turkey are equally good in this hearty salad. This is one to make additions to throughout the week or serve for a quick and cool dinner.

1 large head romaine or lettuce of your choice, shredded
2 cups sliced or diced cooked meat
¼ cup chopped or sliced onion
¼ cup chopped green pepper
1 can (8 ounces) kidney beans, drained
1 large tomato, chopped
½ cup hot taco sauce or salsa

1¼ cups broken tortilla chips
1 cup shredded sharp Cheddar or farmer's cheese
¾ cup no-salt Mexican table sauce
¼ cup safflower oil
½ teaspoon garlic powder
¼ teaspoon minced cilantro or parsley
¼ teaspoon oregano leaves

Line a salad bowl with lettuce. In a bowl, combine meat, onion, green pepper, kidney beans, and tomato. Stir in taco sauce. Spoon meat mixture over lettuce. Sprinkle with tortilla chips and cheese. Combine remaining ingredients. Serve with salad.

NUTRITIONAL INFORMATION PER SERVING

Calories 626	Saturated Fat 14.1g	Fiber 2.11g	Potassium 908mg
Protein 30.4g	Cholesterol 77mg	Calcium 289mg	Sodium 353mg
Total Fat 43.2g	Carbohydrates 29.4g	Iron 4.9mg	

Breast of Smoked Turkey Salad, 41

Seafood Stuffed Tomatoes

Makes 4 servings

Ring seafood stuffed tomatoes with sprouts and shredded carrots for a delightfully different stuffed tomato.

2 large, ripe tomatoes
4 ounces flaked crab meat
1 grapefruit, peeled, segmented, and diced
1 carrot, peeled and shredded
1 cup fresh bean sprouts

¼ cup Herb Vinaigrette Dressing (recipe on page 49)
16 to 20 small leaves curly chicory or escarole
8 to 12 cooked small shrimp
Minced chervil or parsley

Cut tomatoes in half in a sawtooth pattern. Twist gently to separate halves. Gently squeeze out seeds; set aside. In a bowl, combine crab meat and grapefruit; divide evenly among tomato halves. Combine carrot and sprouts with vinaigrette; set aside. Arrange chicory on a large platter or individual serving plates. Place tomatoes in the center. Arrange carrot and sprouts around tomatoes. Sprinkle shrimp over tomatoes. Sprinkle with additional vinaigrette, if desired. Garnish with chervil.

NUTRITIONAL INFORMATION PER SERVING

Calories	159	Saturated Fat	0.8g	Fiber	1.15g	Potassium	477mg
Protein	9.2g	Cholesterol	41mg	Calcium	66mg	Sodium	38mg
Total Fat	7.7g	Carbohydrates	16.1g	Iron	1.9mg		

Crab Louis Salad

Makes 4 servings

½ cup Minceur Mayonnaise (recipe on page 42)
½ cup plain yogurt
¼ cup half-and-half
¼ cup chili sauce
1 teaspoon Worcestershire sauce
1 clove garlic, minced
Dash hot pepper sauce

2 tablespoons lemon juice
¼ cup minced green pepper
¼ cup minced onion
2 cups shredded iceberg lettuce
1 to 2 cups flaked crab meat or cooked small shrimp

In a bowl, combine all ingredients except the lettuce and crab meat. Blend well. Arrange lettuce in a salad bowl. Arrange crab meat over lettuce. Drizzle dressing over crab meat and lettuce.

NUTRITIONAL INFORMATION PER SERVING

Calories	259	Saturated Fat	4.1g	Fiber	0.61g	Potassium	253mg
Protein	17.4g	Cholesterol	159mg	Calcium	113mg	Sodium	344mg
Total Fat	16.5g	Carbohydrates	12.4g	Iron	1.3mg		

Breast of Smoked Turkey Salad

Makes 8 servings

This salad works equally well with smoked or plain cooked chicken or duck.
Vary the nuts or fruit at will for a "signature salad."

4 cups shredded smoked or plain
  cooked turkey
2 ribs celery, sliced
½ cup chopped red onion
¾ cup chopped walnuts or sliced almonds
2 small tart green apples, cored and diced
¼ cup raisins

¼ cup chutney
4 ounces Neufchatel cheese
¼ cup plain yogurt
1 tablespoon lemon juice
1 to 2 teaspoons Dijon-style mustard
  Cayenne pepper to taste

In a large serving bowl, combine first 5 ingredients. In a small bowl, stir together remaining ingredients except cayenne. Pour dressing over salad; mix lightly. Season with cayenne. Refrigerate until chilled.

NUTRITIONAL INFORMATION PER SERVING

Calories 274	Saturated Fat 2.5g	Fiber 0.71g	Potassium 440mg
Protein 5.9g	Cholesterol 55mg	Calcium 58mg	Sodium 146mg
Total Fat 12.1g	Carbohydrates 18.2g	Iron 1.6mg	

Wilted Spinach Wok Salad

Makes 4 servings

1 tablespoon safflower oil
1 tablespoon white wine vinegar or lemon juice
1 to 2 teaspoons Dijon-style mustard
½ teaspoon oregano leaves
2 cloves garlic, minced or pressed
  Salt and freshly ground pepper to taste
1 small red onion, thinly sliced and
  separated into rings

½ pound mushrooms, thinly sliced
2 carrots, peeled and thinly sliced
1 bunch spinach, stemmed, washed, and
  torn into pieces
1 tomato, cut in wedges
¼ cup pitted ripe olives, halved or sliced
⅓ cup walnut pieces

In a wok or large skillet, combine oil, vinegar, mustard, oregano, garlic, salt, and pepper; stir-fry over medium-low heat for about 2 minutes. Add onion, mushrooms, and carrots; stir-fry for 1 minute. Add remaining ingredients; stir-fry for 30 seconds. Serve at once.

NUTRITIONAL INFORMATION PER SERVING

Calories 164	Saturated Fat 1.0g	Fiber 1.63g	Potassium 647mg
Protein 5.2g	Cholesterol 0mg	Calcium 73mg	Sodium 142mg
Total Fat 12.0g	Carbohydrates 17.4g	Iron 2.3mg	

Summer Salad Board

Makes 4 servings

The original recipe was developed for the National Restaurant Association convention in Chicago. The natural flavors are especially enhanced by the Watercress Mayonnaise Dip.

Lettuce leaves
Watercress Mayonnaise Dip
2 cups sliced fresh peaches
2 cups sliced fresh pears

1 fresh pineapple, cut into 1-inch chunks
1 pint fresh strawberries
10 to 12 frozen cooked shrimp, thawed
2 cups broccoli flowerets

Line a large serving platter with lettuce leaves. Place a bowl with Watercress Mayonnaise Dip in the center of the tray. Arrange fruit, shrimp, and broccoli on lettuce. Provide wooden picks or small forks for dipping.

Watercress Mayonnaise Dip

1 bunch watercress, minced
3 tablespoons lemon juice
¼ teaspoon tarragon leaves

1 clove garlic, minced
1 cup Minceur Mayonnaise (recipe below)

In a small bowl, combine all ingredients; blend well.

Minceur Mayonnaise

Makes 1 cup

2 egg yolks
1 tablespoon Dijon-style mustard
2 teaspoons white wine vinegar or lemon juice

½ cup safflower oil
½ cup Neufchatel cheese or kefir
Salt and freshly ground pepper to taste

Combine egg yolks and mustard in a blender or food processor. With motor running, slowly add vinegar drop by drop. Drizzle in oil, slowly increasing flow to a slow, steady stream. Blend in cheese. Season with salt and pepper.

NUTRITIONAL INFORMATION PER SERVING (2 tablespoons)

Calories ... 116	Saturated Fat ... 2.5g	Fiber ... 0.00g	Potassium ... 16.6mg
Protein ... 1.4g	Cholesterol ... 52mg	Calcium ... 13mg	Sodium ... 78mg
Total Fat ... 12.2g	Carbohydrates ... .43g	Iron ... 0.2mg	

Wild Rice Salad

Makes 6 servings

The wild rice can be combined with long-grain white rice in any proportion you desire.
Many of the variations can be combined with other rices or pasta.
Do use your imagination and leftovers!

4 cups cooked wild rice
1½ cups diced, cooked or smoked chicken,
   turkey, or ham
2 cups seedless grapes, halved or whole
½ cup unsalted cashew nuts or sliced almonds

1 cup frozen cooked artichoke hearts,
   chopped
¼ cup plain yogurt
¼ cup sour half-and-half or Neufchatel cheese

In a medium bowl, mix all ingredients gently but thoroughly. Serve at room temperature or chilled.

NUTRITIONAL INFORMATION PER SERVING

Calories	250	Saturated Fat	3.2g	Fiber	1.01g	Potassium	306mg
Protein	15.3g	Cholesterol	35mg	Calcium	37mg	Sodium	80mg
Total Fat	10.4g	Carbohydrates	25.2g	Iron	1.8mg		

Variations

- **Tropical Rice**   Stir ½ cup chutney into yogurt and sour half-and-half. Add 1 can (8 ounces) drained pineapple chunks to rice. Garnish with coconut and raisins.
- **Seafood Rice**   Omit meat, grapes, nuts, and artichokes. Substitute cooked shrimp or crab for meat. Add sliced green onions, tomato wedges, and chopped hard-cooked egg.
- **Minted Rice**   Omit grapes and nuts. Add ½ cup fresh chopped mint and ½ cup minced parsley.
- **Cheese and Rice**   Omit meat, grapes, and nuts. Add ½ cup shredded mozzarella and ½ cup shredded Longhorn Cheddar cheese, 1 can (8 ounces) drained water chestnuts, chopped, and 2 teaspoons lemon juice. Garnish with minced parsley.

Overleaf: (Clockwise from upper left) Vinaigrette Bonne Femme, 49;
Herb French Dressing, 49; Quick-Change Dressing, 48;
Watercress Mayonnaise, 48; Dilled Cheese Dressing, 48

Vegetables Vinaigrette

Makes 6 servings

This is great to make as a party vegetable sampler or to keep on hand in the refrigerator for quick and healthy snacking. This dressing is particularly low in calories because chicken broth is used for part of the oil.

2 to 3 pounds asparagus, ends trimmed,
  or any vegetable combination
2 tablespoons white wine vinegar
2 tablespoons lemon juice
⅛ to ¼ teaspoon salt
1 teaspoon Dijon-style mustard
⅛ teaspoon white pepper

⅛ teaspoon tarragon leaves or dillweed
½ cup safflower oil
¼ cup Chicken Broth (recipe on page 121)
  Red leaf or curly green lettuce leaves
2 hard-cooked eggs, chopped
1 tablespoon chopped parsley
1 tablespoon chopped chives

Steam vegetables over boiling water until tender-crisp. Drain well. In a small bowl, combine vinegar, lemon juice, salt, mustard, pepper, and tarragon. Gradually beat in oil and chicken broth until well blended and smooth. Place a lettuce leaf in each of six shallow au gratin dishes. Arrange warm vegetables on lettuce. Stir dressing and pour evenly over each serving. Garnish with shredded hard-cooked eggs, parsley, and chives.

NUTRITIONAL INFORMATION PER SERVING

Calories 226	Saturated Fat 2.2g	Fiber 1.18g	Potassium 378mg
Protein 5.9g	Cholesterol 91mg	Calcium 58mg	Sodium 107mg
Total Fat 20.5g	Carbohydrates 7.3g	Iron 1.7mg	

Golden Corn Salad

Makes 6 servings

2 cans (8¾ ounces each) whole kernel corn,
  drained
1 can (15 ounces) garbanzo beans, drained
1 can (16 ounces) tomato wedges, drained
⅔ cup chopped green onion or
  2 green peppers, chopped

1 can (4½ ounces) sliced ripe olives
Vinaigrette Bonne Femme (recipe on
page 49)
Endive or romaine leaves

In a serving bowl, stir together first five ingredients. Prepare vinaigrette; toss with salad. Serve on endive leaves. Garnish as desired.

NUTRITIONAL INFORMATION PER SERVING (INCLUDES 2 TABLESPOONS DRESSING)

Calories 255	Saturated Fat 1.1g	Fiber 2.52g	Potassium 513mg
Protein 8.2g	Cholesterol 0mg	Calcium 80mg	Sodium 450mg
Total Fat 11.6g	Carbohydrates 36.6g	Iron 3.2mg	

Vegetables Vinaigrette, this page

Quick-Change Dressing

Makes 1 cup

½ cup plain yogurt
½ cup sour half-and-half or Neufchatel cheese
1 to 2 teaspoons lemon juice

¼ to ½ teaspoon curry powder or
tarragon leaves
Skim milk

In a small bowl, blend all ingredients. Thin with milk, if necessary.

NUTRITIONAL INFORMATION PER SERVING (2 tablespoons)

Calories	47	Saturated Fat	2.42g	Fiber	.013g	Potassium	45mg
Protein	2g	Cholesterol	13mg	Calcium	31.8mg	Sodium	64mg
Total Fat	3.8g	Carbohydrates	1.3g	Iron	.03mg		

Variations

- **Roquefort Dressing** Omit curry and tarragon. Add crumbled Roquefort or blue cheese to taste, 1 clove minced garlic, and 2 thinly sliced green onions.
- **Anchovy Dressing** Omit curry and tarragon. Add 1 tablespoon anchovy paste.
- **Caviar and Capers** Omit curry and tarragon. Substitute onion juice for lemon juice. Add 2 teaspoons capers and ¼ cup red or black caviar.
- **Curried Fruit Dressing** Add 2 tablespoons lemon juice and 1 to 2 teaspoons sugar or honey.
- **Dilled Cheese Dressing** Substitute cottage cheese for Neufchatel and dillweed for curry powder. Add sliced green onion or minced parsley.

Watercress Mayonnaise

Makes 1⅓ cups

1 egg
2 tablespoons white wine vinegar
  or lemon juice
½ cup watercress sprigs
½ cup parsley sprigs
1 green onion, sliced

2 teaspoons Dijon-style mustard
½ teaspoon tarragon leaves
½ cup safflower oil
½ cup Neufchatel cheese or kefir
Salt and freshly ground pepper to taste

In a blender or food processor, combine first 7 ingredients; blend until smooth. With machine running, add oil, a few drops at a time, increasing flow to a slow, steady stream. Blend in cheese and season with salt and pepper.

NUTRITIONAL INFORMATION PER SERVING (2 tablespoons)

Calories	131	Saturated Fat	2.6g	Fiber	0.09g	Potassium	60.25mg
Protein	2.0g	Cholesterol	34mg	Calcium	26.8mg	Sodium	115mg
Total Fat	13.4g	Carbohydrates	1.2g	Iron	.43mg		

Vinaigrette Bonne Femme
Makes 2 cups

½ cup safflower oil
½ cup olive oil
⅓ to ½ cup white or red wine vinegar
   or lemon juice
1 tablespoon Dijon-style mustard

¼ teaspoon salt
¼ teaspoon freshly ground pepper
3 or 4 cloves garlic, minced or pressed
½ teaspoon oregano leaves
¼ teaspoon thyme leaves

Combine all ingredients in a stoppered jar or cruet. Shake until blended. Let stand until slightly thickened. Taste and adjust seasonings. If dressing is too sharp, add ½ to 1 teaspoon sugar. If dressing is too oily-tasting, add a small amount of salt.

NUTRITIONAL INFORMATION PER SERVING

Calories 122	Saturated Fat 1.5g	Fiber 0.03g	Potassium 13mg
Protein 0.1g	Cholesterol 0mg	Calcium 3.6mg	Sodium 46mg
Total Fat 13.6g	Carbohydrates 2.4g	Iron 0.1mg	

Variations

- **Herb Vinaigrette**   Increase herbs to 1 heaping tablespoon. Try different combinations of mixed chopped herbs.
- **Parsley and Shallot Vinaigrette**   Omit thyme and oregano. Substitute 3 tablespoons minced fresh parsley and 1 or 2 minced shallots or green onions. Add 1 or 2 soft-cooked (3½-minute) eggs: blend yolks into the vinaigrette; chop the whites and stir into dressing.
- Substitute ½ cup chicken broth for the olive oil.

Herb French Dressing
Makes 1 cup

4 ounces Neufchatel cheese, softened
1 to 2 teaspoons minced onion
½ teaspoon dry mustard
½ teaspoon crushed basil
½ teaspoon paprika

2 to 3 tablespoons minced parsley
¼ cup safflower oil
1½ tablespoons vinegar
1½ tablespoons water

In a blender or food processor, combine cheese, onion, mustard, basil, paprika, and parsley; blend well. With machine running, gradually add oil, vinegar, and water; blend until smooth.

NUTRITIONAL INFORMATION PER SERVING (2 tablespoons)

Calories 100	Saturated Fat 2.7g	Fiber 0.08g	Potassium 37.5mg
Protein 1.5g	Cholesterol 11mg	Calcium 15.7mg	Sodium 57.3mg
Total Fat 10.0g	Carbohydrates 1.0g	Iron .... .16mg	

MEAT

African Bobotie
Makes 8 servings

1 tablespoon butter or safflower oil, divided
¼ cup sliced almonds
1 large red onion, chopped
1 tart green apple, diced
1 tablespoon curry powder
2 pounds lean ground beef
½ cup fine dry bread crumbs
2 eggs, divided

1½ cups skim milk, divided
2 tablespoons vinegar
2 tablespoons low-sugar apricot jam
   or orange marmalade
½ teaspoon salt
¼ teaspoon freshly ground pepper
6 bay leaves

In a large skillet, heat half of the butter. Add almonds; cook and stir over medium heat until lightly browned. Remove almonds from skillet; set aside. Add remaining butter, onion, and apple to skillet; cook, stirring occasionally, about 10 minutes or until onion is tender. Stir in curry; cook 1 minute. Remove from heat; let stand about 3 minutes. Add ground beef, bread crumbs, 1 egg, ½ cup skim milk, vinegar, jam, salt, pepper, and almonds; blend well. Pack beef mixture into a shallow oval or rectangular 13 x 9-inch baking dish. Arrange bay leaves on top. Bake, uncovered, at 375° F. for 40 minutes. Lightly beat together the remaining 1 egg and 1 cup milk. Remove baking dish from oven. Carefully pour egg mixture over top of loaf. Return to oven for 10 minutes.

NUTRITIONAL INFORMATION PER SERVING

Calories	314	Saturated Fat	7.0g	Fiber	0.62g	Potassium	578mg
Protein	28.1g	Cholesterol	152mg	Calcium	106mg	Sodium	288mg
Total Fat	16.9g	Carbohydrates	10.9g	Iron	4.6mg		

Mexicali Pork Stir-Fry, 53

Lamb Chops with Coriander

Makes 8 servings

This is a low-calorie variation of a Cordon Bleu classic.

4 or 5 cloves garlic, minced or pressed
1 tablespoon ground coriander
8 loin lamb chops, fat trimmed
1 small red onion, sliced

½ cup white wine
½ cup Chicken Broth (recipe on page 121)
2 teaspoons arrowroot flour, optional
1 tablespoon water, optional

Rub garlic and coriander over both sides of chops. Place chops in a roasting pan. Cover with onion slices. Pour wine and broth over and around chops. Bake at 400° F. for 30 to 45 minutes or until done. Transfer chops to a warm serving platter. Reduce liquid in roasting pan over high heat to make a sauce. If a thicker sauce is desired, dissolve arrowroot in water and stir into sauce. Bring just to boiling, stirring constantly. Pour sauce over chops and serve.

NUTRITIONAL INFORMATION PER SERVING

Calories	145	Saturated Fat	2.7g	Fiber	0.13g	Potassium	264mg
Protein	18.9g	Cholesterol	45mg	Calcium	16mg	Sodium	53mg
Total Fat	5.0g	Carbohydrates	7.2g	Iron	1.6mg		

Variations

• **Delicate Wine Sauce**   Omit sauce ingredients. Substitute:

¼ cup minced shallots or green onion
¼ cup tarragon vinegar
½ cup dry red wine
½ cup Chicken Broth (recipe on page 121)
½ teaspoon tarragon leaves

2 large mushrooms, minced
2 tablespoons minced watercress leaves
2 teaspoons arrowroot flour
2 tablespoons water
2 dashes cayenne pepper

In a heavy enamel saucepan, combine shallots and vinegar. Cook, uncovered, over medium heat until liquid is reduced, about 3 minutes. Add wine, broth, and tarragon. Simmer for 4 minutes. Strain into a bowl, pressing out liquid. Return strained sauce to saucepan. Add mushrooms and watercress; simmer for 2 minutes. Dissolve arrowroot in water. Gradually stir into sauce. Add cayenne. Cook and stir until slightly thickened.

• **Lemon Vermouth Sauce**   Omit garlic, coriander, and white wine. Substitute:

1 teaspoon grated lemon peel
1 teaspoon orange juice concentrate

½ cup dry vermouth
2 tablespoons minced dillweed or mint leaves

Add lemon peel, orange juice, and vermouth with the broth. Garnish chops with dillweed or mint.

Mexicali Pork Stir-Fry

Makes 4 servings

1 tablespoon safflower oil
1 pound pork tenderloin, cut into chunks
1 red onion, diced
2 or 3 green onions, sliced
2 or 3 cloves garlic, minced or pressed
¼ cup lime juice

1 cup Beef Broth (recipe on page 121)
¼ cup diced tomatoes
1 tablespoon tomato paste
1 tablespoon paprika
1 tablespoon minced cilantro or parsley
1 or 2 green tomatilloes or red salsa

In a large skillet or wok, heat oil. Stir-fry pork chunks, onions, and garlic until onions are tender and pork is browned. Stir in remaining ingredients; simmer 15 to 20 minutes. Reduce cooking liquid to desired consistency for sauce over high heat.

NUTRITIONAL INFORMATION PER SERVING

Calories	213	Saturated Fat	1.9g	Fiber	0.75g	Potassium	724mg
Protein	27.5g	Cholesterol	86mg	Calcium	31mg	Sodium	74mg
Total Fat	8.0g	Carbohydrates	12.1g	Iron	2.3mg		

Veal with Lemon Spinach

Makes 4 servings

2 tablespoons safflower oil
1½ pounds veal stew meat, cut in 1-inch cubes
  Freshly ground pepper to taste
1 large red onion, chopped
1½ cups Chicken Broth (recipe on page 121)

½ teaspoon crushed fennel seed
3 or 4 small green onions, chopped
2 packages (10 ounces each) frozen spinach leaves
Lemon wedges

Heat oil in a Dutch oven or large saucepan. Brown veal evenly on all sides. Season with pepper. Add onion and sauté until limp but not brown. Add broth and fennel seed. Cover and simmer about 45 minutes or until veal is tender, adding additional broth or water, if necessary. Add green onions and spinach. Cover and simmer just until spinach is tender, 5 to 10 minutes. Season to taste. Arrange veal on a serving platter. Arrange a border of spinach around veal. Garnish with lemon wedges.

NUTRITIONAL INFORMATION PER SERVING

Calories	396	Saturated Fat	9.1g	Fiber	1.35g	Potassium	1124mg
Protein	40.1g	Cholesterol	108mg	Calcium	175mg	Sodium	214mg
Total Fat	21.3g	Carbohydrates	12.6g	Iron	8.8mg		

Broiled Beef

Makes 4 servings

**Artichoke Béarnaise, Herb Butter,
or Tomato Barbecue Sauce**

4 beef filet mignon steaks, 1½ to 2 inches thick

Prepare sauce of your choice. Preheat broiler. Broil steaks about 4 inches from heat source 7 to 8 minutes on each side (rare) or longer if desired. Spoon sauce over steaks and serve.

NUTRITIONAL INFORMATION PER SERVING

Calories	236	Saturated Fat	4.1g	Fiber	0.00g	Potassium	413mg
Protein	36.8g	Cholesterol	79mg	Calcium	14mg	Sodium	90mg
Total Fat	8.7g	Carbohydrates	0.0g	Iron	4.4mg		

Artichoke Béarnaise

4 artichoke bottoms
¼ cup red wine
¼ cup red wine vinegar
1 teaspoon tarragon leaves

1 teaspoon minced green onion
¼ cup butter, melted
¾ cup Neufchatel cheese or kefir
Yellow food coloring, optional

Before broiling steaks, cook artichoke bottoms in hot water until tender. Drain and set aside. In a small saucepan, bring wine, vinegar, tarragon, and onion to a boil. Blend in butter and Neufchatel. Add food coloring as desired.

Herb Butter

¼ cup butter
1 tablespoon lemon juice
2 tablespoons chopped parsley

2 tablespoons chopped watercress
½ teaspoon Worcestershire sauce
Dash white pepper

At least 3 hours before broiling steaks, prepare Herb Butter. In a small mixing bowl, cream butter until light and fluffy. Gradually add remaining ingredients; blend well. Shape into a roll; wrap in plastic wrap. Chill at least 3 hours or until firm. Top broiled steaks with 1 teaspoon to 1 tablespoon butter.

Tomato Barbecue Sauce

1 teaspoon safflower oil
1 medium onion, chopped
1 clove garlic, minced
½ teaspoon chili powder
¼ teaspoon dry mustard

1 tablespoon brown sugar
3 tablespoons cider vinegar
1 tablespoon Worcestershire sauce
¾ cup low-sodium tomato sauce
¾ cup dry red wine

In a medium saucepan, heat oil. Sauté onion until tender. Stir in remaining ingredients. Stir until sugar dissolves and mixture begins to boil. Reduce heat; simmer 3 to 5 minutes. Spoon over steaks.

Broiled Beef, this page

Baked Chops with Apples and Onions

Makes 4 servings

4 center-cut rib pork chops, well trimmed;
 reserve 1 large piece fat
1 large onion, cut in 8 slices

¼ cup Vegetable or Beef Broth (recipes
 on pages 114 and 121)
Madeira or port wine
1 medium green apple, cored and cut in 4 rings

Lightly grease a large skillet with pork fat. Brown chops on both sides. Place 2 onion slices on each chop. Pour in broth. Cover and simmer 20 minutes, adding additional broth or water if necessary. Place an apple ring on each chop. Cover and cook 10 minutes or until chops are tender and no longer pink.

NUTRITIONAL INFORMATION PER SERVING

Calories	195	Saturated Fat	2.6g	Fiber	0.59g	Potassium	373mg
Protein	19.0g	Cholesterol	51mg	Calcium	23mg	Sodium	99mg
Total Fat	7.8g	Carbohydrates	9.8g	Iron	1.0mg		

Variations

• **Cranberry Cumberland Sauce** Omit onion, broth, and apple. Add:

1 can (16 ounces) low-sugar whole berry
 cranberry sauce
¼ cup port wine
¼ cup orange juice
½ teaspoon grated lemon peel

½ teaspoon grated orange peel
½ teaspoon ground ginger
1 teaspoon arrowroot or cornstarch, optional
1 tablespoon cold water, optional

Combine cranberry sauce, wine, orange juice, fruit peels, and ginger. Pour over chops in skillet. Cover and simmer 30 to 45 minutes or until chops are tender and no longer pink. If a thicker sauce is desired, dissolve arrowroot in cold water; stir into sauce. Cook and stir until thickened.

• **Madeira Sauce** Omit onion, broth, and apple. Add:

1 teaspoon butter
⅔ cup sliced mushrooms
1 cup Chicken Broth (recipe on page 121)
⅓ cup Madeira wine

2 teaspoons tomato paste
1 teaspoon arrowroot or cornstarch
1 tablespoon cold water

In a small saucepan, melt butter. Sauté mushrooms until tender. Add chicken broth and wine. Blend in tomato paste. Dissolve arrowroot in cold water. Stir into sauce and simmer 10 minutes. Pour over chops in skillet. Cover and simmer 30 to 45 minutes or until chops are tender and no longer pink.

Indian Keema

Makes 4 servings

The addition of unusual spices makes this an interesting variation on the meat and potatoes theme.

1 teaspoon safflower oil
1 large red onion, finely chopped
1¼ teaspoons cumin seed
4 medium potatoes, peeled (about 1 pound)
1 tablespoon minced garlic
2 tablespoons minced ginger root
1½ pounds lean ground lamb or beef
1 teaspoon cardamom

½ teaspoon cinnamon
¼ teaspoon cayenne pepper or crushed red pepper flakes
⅛ teaspoon cloves
⅔ cup plain yogurt
½ cup skim milk
½ to ¾ teaspoon salt, optional

In a heavy skillet, heat oil. Add onion; cook over medium-low heat, stirring often, for about 15 minutes or until onion is golden brown. While onion is cooking, toast cumin seed in a separate skillet, shaking the skillet until cumin is lightly browned. Remove seed from skillet; set aside. Cut potatoes in halves; cover with cold water and set aside. Add garlic and ginger root to onions; cook about 2 minutes, stirring constantly. Add ground meat; cook until no longer pink, stirring and breaking up with a spoon. Drain potatoes; add to meat mixture. Add spices, yogurt, and milk. Bring to a boil; cover and simmer 30 to 45 minutes, stirring occasionally, until potatoes are tender. Remove from heat. Add cumin seed; stir gently.

NUTRITIONAL INFORMATION PER SERVING

Calories 374	Saturated Fat 4.0g	Fiber 1.33g	Potassium 1060mg
Protein 35.2g	Cholesterol 76mg	Calcium 132mg	Sodium 445mg
Total Fat 10.0g	Carbohydrates 41.4g	Iron 4.0mg	

———————————————— Variation ————————————————

- **Keema with Tomatoes and Peas**   Add to meat mixture with potatoes:

1 cup peas
1 cup diced tomatoes
1 tablespoon lime juice

1 teaspoon curry powder
½ teaspoon turmeric
¼ teaspoon coriander seed

POULTRY

Chicken Parisienne

Makes 6 servings

*It's always a delight to dine on a continental dish that does
not include excess calories, cholesterol, or cream.*

3 whole chicken breasts, halved
1 red onion, diced
1 cup Chicken Broth (recipe on page 121)
¼ cup dry sherry
**½ teaspoon grated or ¼ teaspoon
   ground nutmeg**
¼ teaspoon cinnamon

Pinch cayenne pepper
Salt and freshly ground pepper to taste
1 tablespoon minced parsley, optional
2 tablespoons flour
½ cup evaporated skim milk
¼ cup skim milk

Brown chicken, skin side down, in an electric skillet. Cook over medium heat until the skin is well browned; drain fat. Turn chicken skin side up. Add onion, broth, and sherry. Sprinkle with seasonings. Cover and simmer over very low heat until almost tender, 40 to 50 minutes. Uncover. Tip pan and skim fat. Simmer, uncovered, until liquid is reduced by half. Combine with evaporated skim milk. Blend flour into milk; stir into pan liquid. Cook and stir until sauce is bubbly and thickened.

NUTRITIONAL INFORMATION PER SERVING

Calories	185	Saturated Fat	0.7g	Fiber	0.17g	Potassium	323mg
Protein	28.2g	Cholesterol	68mg	Calcium	95mg	Sodium	144mg
Total Fat	2.9g	Carbohydrates	7.0g	Iron	1.3mg		

Chicken Sauté Orangerie, 65

Fast Baked Chicken

Makes 4 servings

1 broiler-fryer chicken (3 to 3½ pounds),
   cut up and trimmed of fat
Salt and freshly ground pepper to taste

1 red onion, chopped
1 cup Chicken Broth (recipe on page 121)

Arrange chicken pieces, skin side up, in a shallow baking pan. Bake at 500° F. for 15 to 20 minutes or until skin is crisp and well rendered of fat; drain fat from pan. Add remaining ingredients to pan. Reduce heat to 350° F. and bake, basting occasionally, until chicken is tender, 15 to 20 minutes. Spoon pan juice over chicken and serve.

NUTRITIONAL INFORMATION PER SERVING

Calories 243	Saturated Fat 2.5g	Fiber 0.18g	Potassium 372mg
Protein 35.9g	Cholesterol 106mg	Calcium 28mg	Sodium 190mg
Total Fat 9.1g	Carbohydrates 2.1g	Iron 1.6mg	

Variations

- **African Chicken**   Season chicken with ⅛ teaspoon ground turmeric. Replace 2 tablespoons of chicken broth with 2 tablespoons lemon juice. Add 1 bay leaf and 2 minced garlic cloves to pan.

- **Chinese Chicken**   Season chicken with garlic powder and ⅛ teaspoon ground ginger or 1 teaspoon minced ginger root. Reduce chicken broth to ¾ cup and add ¼ cup dry sherry and 2 tablespoons mild soy sauce.

- **French Chicken**   Season chicken with a pinch of grated nutmeg and a dash of poultry seasoning or sage. After browning chicken, place 2 sliced carrots, 1 sliced celery rib and 1 cup sliced mushrooms under chicken in pan. Reduce broth to ¾ cup and add ¼ cup dry white wine.

- **Czechoslovakian Chicken**   Season chicken with 1 tablespoon paprika, 2 to 3 minced garlic cloves and a generous pinch of coriander seed. Reduce chicken broth to ½ cup. Add ½ cup tomato juice and 2 tablespoons dry white wine.

- **Italian Chicken**   Season chicken with 1 teaspoon crushed oregano and 1 teaspoon crushed basil. Add 1 seeded and diced green or red pepper and 2 minced garlic cloves. Replace broth with ¾ cup tomato juice and ¼ cup dry red wine. Before serving, sprinkle with 2 to 3 tablespoons grated Romano or Parmesan cheese.

Chicken Adrienne

Makes 4 servings

2 teaspoons safflower oil
3 medium cloves garlic, mashed
1 red onion, sliced or diced
1 green pepper, sliced
½ pound mushrooms, sliced
1 can (28 ounces) Italian-style tomatoes
2 tablespoons minced parsley

2 teaspoons oregano leaves
2 teaspoons basil leaves
½ teaspoon anise seed
1 large bay leaf
1 broiler-fryer chicken (3 to 3½ pounds),
   cut up and skinned
Salt and freshly ground pepper to taste

In a large skillet, heat oil. Add garlic, onion, green pepper, and mushrooms. Cook over medium heat, stirring often, until onion is tender, about 5 minutes. Add tomatoes, parsley, oregano, basil, anise seed, and bay leaf. Add chicken pieces. Season with salt and pepper. Simmer for 30 to 45 minutes or until chicken is tender. Remove chicken to a serving platter. Spoon sauce over chicken.

NUTRITIONAL INFORMATION PER SERVING

Calories 343	Saturated Fat 2.8g	Fiber 1.98g	Potassium 1121mg
Protein 41.5g	Cholesterol 116mg	Calcium 65mg	Sodium 465mg
Total Fat 12.6g	Carbohydrates 22.0g	Iron 3.8mg	

Variations

• **Coq au Vin**   Omit oil, tomatoes, oregano, and anise. Substitute:

4 ounces Canadian bacon, diced
⅓ cup dry red wine

1 teaspoon marjoram leaves
1 package (10 ounces) frozen pearl onions

Sauté Canadian bacon with chicken until golden brown; drain fat. Blot chicken with paper towels. Add wine, marjoram, and onions; simmer until tender.

• **Poulet Provencale**   Omit oregano and anise. Substitute:

1 carrot, thinly sliced
¼ to ⅓ cup sherry

1 teaspoon thyme leaves

Sauté carrot with chicken; drain fat. Blot chicken with paper towels. Add sherry and thyme; simmer until tender.

Scallopini alla Marsala

Makes 4 servings

This exemplifies the possibilities of making an inexpensive, easy, and elegant variation of a classic dish.

1½ pounds turkey cutlets (sliced from boned turkey breast)
2 teaspoons butter
2 teaspoons safflower oil

½ cup Marsala wine
2 tablespoons Chicken Broth (recipe on page 121)
Minced parsley

Pound turkey cutlets between pieces of waxed paper or plastic wrap until very thin. In a large skillet, heat butter and oil. Brown turkey slices well on both sides over high heat, about 4 minutes total. Add wine and cook over high heat 1 minute. Remove turkey to a serving dish. Deglaze pan with chicken broth over high heat. Pour sauce over turkey. Garnish with parsley.

NUTRITIONAL INFORMATION PER SERVING

Calories	278	Saturated Fat	2.7g	Fiber	0.03g	Potassium	427mg
Protein	4.5g	Cholesterol	91mg	Calcium	31mg	Sodium	126mg
Total Fat	8.3g	Carbohydrates	3.4g	Iron	2.2mg		

Variations

- **Champignons** Add sliced fresh mushrooms after cutlets have been browned on first side.
- **Saltimbocca** Sauté cutlets. Top each with 1 slice Westphalian or Black Forest ham and 1 slice farmer's, mozzarella, or Provolone cheese.
- **Parmigiana** Sauté cutlets. Place a layer of cutlets in a 13 x 9-inch baking dish. Top with ½ cup tomato sauce and ½ cup grated Parmesan or shredded farmer's cheese. Layer remaining cutlets, overlapping slightly, with more tomato sauce and cheese. Bake at 500° F. for 3 to 5 minutes or until bubbly and golden.

Scallopini alla Marsala, this page

Grilled Gingered Chicken

Makes 4 servings

Barbecued, broiled, or grilled, this makes an excellent entree. Try the Teriyaki or Herbed Lemon Marinades for two more delicious alternatives!

2 whole chicken breasts, boned and skinned
2 tablespoons soy sauce
¼ cup lemon juice
1 tablespoon honey
1 teaspoon minced ginger root or ¼ teaspoon ground ginger

8 small white onions
8 to 16 large mushrooms
1 zucchini squash, sliced in rounds
1 crookneck squash, sliced in rounds

Soak eight 8-inch bamboo skewers in water to cover for 30 minutes. Cut chicken breasts into 1-inch chunks. In a bowl, combine soy sauce, lemon juice, honey, and ginger root. Add chicken; toss to coat with marinade. Preheat broiler or start grill. Bring a medium saucepan of water to a boil. Add onions; cook 5 minutes. Drain and rinse with cold water. Cut each onion into 4 wedges. Drain chicken; reserve marinade. Alternately thread chicken, mushrooms, onion wedges, and squash onto skewers. Broil kebabs on a rack in broiler pan or grill about 5 inches from heat source for 5 minutes on each side. Brush with reserved marinade during broiling time.

NUTRITIONAL INFORMATION PER SERVING

Calories	285	Saturated Fat	1.2g	Fiber	1.62g	Potassium	935mg
Protein	43.0g	Cholesterol	105mg	Calcium	69mg	Sodium	622mg
Total Fat	4.9g	Carbohydrates	17.0g	Iron	2.6mg		

Variations

- Cut 1 green pepper into 1½-inch pieces. Skewer green pepper along with onion, chicken, and halved cherry tomatoes.

- To serve as an appetizer, omit mushrooms and squash. Thread 1 piece chicken, 1 piece onion, and 1 piece green pepper on long party toothpicks or sandwich picks. Broil as above.

- **Mustard and Herb Kebabs**   Omit all sauce ingredients. Substitute:

⅓ cup safflower oil
¼ cup dry white wine
1 tablespoon red wine vinegar
1 tablespoon lemon juice
2 cloves garlic, minced or pressed
1½ tablespoons Dijon-style mustard
¼ teaspoon salt

¼ teaspoon fructose or sugar
⅛ teaspoon thyme leaves
⅛ teaspoon basil leaves
⅛ teaspoon oregano leaves
⅛ teaspoon tarragon leaves
Dash freshly ground pepper

In a blender or food processor, combine all ingredients; blend until smooth. Use as marinade for chicken as above.

Chicken Sauté Orangerie

Makes 4 servings

Turkey breasts lend themselves extremely well to this flash-in-the-pan sauté. You can vary the sauces and garnishes and come up with a multitude of meals.

2 chicken breasts, halved, boned, and skinned
½ cup flour
2 to 3 cloves garlic, minced or pressed
2 teaspoons butter
2 teaspoons safflower oil
Grated peel of 2 oranges

1 cup orange juice
¼ cup minced parsley
¼ cup dry white wine
2 oranges, peeled and sliced
3 tablespoons Fini Balsamic vinegar or other white vinegar

Pound chicken breasts between sheets of waxed paper or plastic wrap to ¼-inch thickness. Combine flour and garlic. Dredge chicken in flour mixture to coat. In a large skillet, heat butter and oil. Sauté chicken until tender and browned on both sides. Add orange peel, orange juice, parsley, and wine. Bring to a simmer. Remove chicken to a serving plate. Garnish with orange slices. Add vinegar to skillet. Reduce sauce on high heat if a thicker sauce is desired. Pour sauce over chicken.

NUTRITIONAL INFORMATION PER SERVING

Calories 306	Saturated Fat 2.1g	Fiber 0.42g	Potassium 498mg
Protein 28.1g	Cholesterol 72mg	Calcium 69mg	Sodium 79mg
Total Fat 7.2g	Carbohydrates 36.1g	Iron 1.8mg	

─── Variations ───

• **Cuban Chicken**   Omit oranges and juice. Substitute:

½ teaspoon paprika
½ bay leaf
Pinch saffron powder

¾ cup chicken broth
¼ cup dark rum

Season chicken with paprika, bay leaf, and saffron. Add broth and rum with wine.

• **Indian Chicken**   Omit oranges and ½ cup orange juice. Substitute:

½ cup chopped red onion
½ cup chopped green pepper or celery
½ cup sliced mushrooms
2 to 3 teaspoons curry powder

¼ teaspoon cinnamon
¼ teaspoon allspice
½ cup chicken broth
¼ cup raisins

Sauté onion, green pepper, and mushrooms with chicken. Season with curry, cinnamon, and allspice. Add chicken broth with wine. Garnish with raisins.

SEAFOOD

Fish with Lemon Orange Thins

Makes 2 servings

Try this novel dish — its flavor is heightened by the addition of piquant cookies!

2 flounder or other fish fillets
⅛ teaspoon salt
1 cup light-style beer
1 bay leaf, broken in half
1 teaspoon lemon juice

⅛ teaspoon fructose or sugar
4 to 5 Lemon Orange Thins (recipe on page 126)
1½ teaspoons flour
1 tablespoon butter

Rinse fish in cold water. Sprinkle with salt. Pour beer into a large skillet. Place fish in skillet. Add bay leaf, lemon juice, and fructose. Cook over medium-high heat until fish flakes easily. If fish begins to break up, reduce heat to low. While fish is cooking, remove ¼ cup of the pan liquid; place in a mixing bowl. Add Lemon Orange Thins, flour, and butter. Mash with a spoon until fairly smooth. Remove fish from pan to a serving platter. Keep warm in oven. Transfer mixture in mixing bowl to skillet. Cook over high heat, stirring constantly until slightly thickened. Serve hot over fish.

NUTRITIONAL INFORMATION PER SERVING

Calories 268	Saturated Fat 5.4g	Fiber 0.04g	Potassium 388mg
Protein 18.4g	Cholesterol 32mg	Calcium 25mg	Sodium 321mg
Total Fat 10.9g	Carbohydrates 16.7g	Iron 1.4mg	

Orange Roughy (variation: Tomato-Cilantro Sauce), 68

Orange Roughy and Mushrooms

Makes 4 servings

2 teaspoons butter, divided
1 teaspoon safflower oil
4 orange roughy fillets (1½ pounds)

¼ cup pine nuts
½ pound mushrooms, sliced
¼ cup Bianco Italian or other white wine

Warm a serving platter in a 200° F. oven. In a large skillet over medium-high heat, melt 1 teaspoon butter with oil. Sauté fillets on both sides, nice sides down first, without crowding. Cook only until fish flakes and is opaque and still moist. Transfer fillets to serving platter and place in oven to keep warm. Wipe skillet clean with paper towels; return to heat. Melt remaining 1 teaspoon butter. Sauté pine nuts until toasted. Add mushrooms and wine; cook over high heat until wine is reduced to 1 to 2 tablespoons. Swirl and pour over fish.

NUTRITIONAL INFORMATION PER SERVING

Calories	247	Saturated Fat	1.4g	Fiber	0.65g	Potassium	830mg
Protein	31.1g	Cholesterol	6mg	Calcium	27mg	Sodium	163mg
Total Fat	10.5g	Carbohydrates	4.2g	Iron	2.3mg		

Variations

• **Celery Root Sauce**   Omit 1 teaspoon butter, pine nuts, mushrooms, and wine. Substitute:

½ cup finely minced celery root or celery
2 tablespoons lemon juice
½ cup plain yogurt

1 tablespoon Dijon-style mustard
Cayenne pepper to taste

Place all ingredients in a blender or food processor. Process only to mix, retaining texture of grated celery.

• **Curry Sauce**   Omit as in variation above. Substitute:

1 tablespoon safflower oil
1 tablespoon chopped shallots or green onion
1 tablespoon curry powder

½ cup plain yogurt
½ banana, cut in chunks

In a skillet, heat oil. Sauté shallots until tender. Stir in curry; cook 3 to 4 minutes, stirring constantly. Transfer to a blender or food processor. Add yogurt and banana; blend until smooth.

• **Tomato-Cilantro Sauce**   Omit as in variation above. Substitute:

2 cups chopped tomatoes
2 or 3 cloves garlic, minced or pressed
1 or 2 tablespoons chopped cilantro

2 teaspoons chopped parsley
1 tablespoon safflower oil
¼ teaspoon freshly ground pepper

In a medium saucepan, combine all ingredients; blend well. Cook over medium heat, stirring occasionally until heated through.

Ginger Baked Fish Steaks

Makes 6 servings

3 to 4 bay leaves, broken up, optional
1 to 2 cloves garlic, minced
4 swordfish, salmon, or other fish steaks,
   about 1 inch thick (1½ pounds)
3 to 4 tablespoons lime juice

Freshly ground pepper and
   paprika to taste
1 to 2 teaspoons minced ginger root
1 lime, thinly sliced
Minced fresh parsley

Place bay leaves and garlic in a shallow baking dish. Arrange fish steaks in a single layer on top. Sprinkle with lime juice, pepper, paprika, and ginger root. Cover and bake at 425° F. for 12 to 20 minutes or until fish flakes easily, basting frequently with pan juices. Garnish with lime slices and parsley.

NUTRITIONAL INFORMATION PER SERVING

Calories 145	Saturated Fat 0.0g	Fiber 0.24g	Potassium 71mg
Protein 22.2g	Cholesterol 80mg	Calcium 38mg	Sodium 47mg
Total Fat 4.6g	Carbohydrates 5.0g	Iron 1.5mg	

Lemon Fish with Curried Rice

Makes 4 servings

1 teaspoon safflower oil
1½ cups brown or white rice
1 rib celery, sliced
¼ cup minced red onion
2 to 3 teaspoons curry powder
1 teaspoon ground ginger

1¾ cups Chicken Broth (recipe on page 121)
1 can (5¼ ounces) pineapple chunks drained;
   reserve juice
¼ cup flaked or grated coconut
4 white fish fillets

In an electric skillet or wok, heat oil to 350° F. Add rice, celery, onion, and spices; cook for 6 to 8 minutes, stirring frequently. Add chicken broth and reserved pineapple juice; bring to a boil. Reduce heat; cover and simmer over low heat for 10 minutes. Add pineapple and coconut to rice. Cover and simmer 10 minutes. Arrange fillets on top of rice; cover and steam 8 to 10 minutes. Serve from wok or skillet.

NUTRITIONAL INFORMATION PER SERVING

Calories 289	Saturated Fat 5.7g	Fiber 0.62g	Potassium 703mg
Protein 21.6g	Cholesterol 0mg	Calcium 43mg	Sodium 127mg
Total Fat 9.3g	Carbohydrates 29.5g	Iron 2.4mg	

Scrod Amandine

Perch with Confetti Garnish

Haddock with Tropical Garnish

Swordfish with Fresh Dill-Cucumber Sauce

Fillets a la Meuniere

Makes 4 servings

Use any low-cost, mild-flavored boneless fillets, such as sea bass, swordfish, turbot, halibut, calamari, cod, snapper, perch, thrasher shark, or orange roughy.

2 teaspoons butter, divided
1 teaspoon safflower oil
1¼ pounds fish fillets
¼ cup butter
¼ cup lemon juice

¼ cup minced parsley
¼ teaspoon thyme leaves
¼ teaspoon basil leaves
¼ teaspoon rosemary leaves

Warm a serving platter in a 200° F. oven. In a large skillet over medium-high heat, melt 1 tablespoon butter and oil. Sauté fillets on both sides, nice side down first, without crowding. Cook only until fish flakes and is opaque and still moist. Remove fillets to serving platter and place in oven to keep warm. Wipe pan clean with paper towels; return to heat. Melt remaining 1 teaspoon butter. When butter is lightly browned and foaming, add lemon juice and herbs all at once. Swirl briefly and pour over fish.

NUTRITIONAL INFORMATION PER SERVING

Calories 271	Saturated Fat 8.4g	Fiber 0.09g	Potassium 52mg
Protein 30.6g	Cholesterol 37mg	Calcium 16mg	Sodium 139mg
Total Fat 15.3g	Carbohydrates 1.7g	Iron 0.4mg	

Variations

- **Fresh Dill-Cucumber Sauce** Omit 1 teaspoon butter, lemon juice, and herbs. Substitute:

½ cucumber, finely diced
½ small red onion, finely diced
½ cup Minceur Mayonnaise (recipe on page 42)

½ cup plain yogurt
2 tablespoons minced fresh dillweed or
  1 to 2 teaspoons dry dillweed

In a bowl, combine all ingredients; blend well. Serve with fillets.

- **Fillets Amandine** Omit as in first variation. Substitute:

1 or 2 tablespoons butter
¼ cup sliced almonds

3 or 4 tablespoons Marsala wine

In a skillet, melt butter. Sauté almonds until golden. Add wine; heat through. Pour sauce over fillets.

- **Confetti Garnish** Omit as in first variation. Garnish fillets with finely chopped sweet red pepper, candied ginger, and minced parsley.

- **Tropical Garnish** Omit as in first variation. Garnish fillets with thinly sliced papaya, kiwi, and banana.

Fillets a la Meuniere, this page

Snapper in Orange Sauce

Makes 2 servings

¾ pound snapper fillets or other firm-fleshed
  moist fish, such as flounder, pompano,
  croaker, sea bass, or orange roughy
Salt and white pepper to taste

1 tablespoon orange juice
1 tablespoon lemon juice
1½ teaspoons grated orange peel
1 tablespoon butter

Heat oven broiler. Place fillets in a foil-lined shallow baking dish. Season with salt and pepper. In a small saucepan, combine orange juice, lemon juice, orange peel, and butter; heat until butter melts. Spoon a little of the sauce over the fillets. Broil fillets 2 inches from heat source, turning once if they have been skinned. Broil 8 to 10 minutes, basting once or twice with orange mixture, until fish flakes easily with a fork.

NUTRITIONAL INFORMATION PER SERVING

Calories	215	Saturated Fat	3.6g	Fiber	0.06g	Potassium	585mg
Protein	33.9g	Cholesterol	101mg	Calcium	35mg	Sodium	306mg
Total Fat	7.3g	Carbohydrates	1.11g	Iron	1.5mg		

Variations

- **Tarragon Butter**   Omit orange juice and peel. Substitute:

  3 tablespoons dry vermouth
  2 tablespoons butter

  ¾ teaspoon tarragon leaves

Broil fillets. Combine all ingredients; blend well. Dot each fillet with about 1 tablespoon butter mixture.

- **Mock Béarnaise Sauce**   Omit orange juice and peel. Substitute:

  2 tablespoons diced shallots or green onions
  ¼ cup dry white wine
  2 tablespoons tarragon red wine vinegar
  ½ cup plain yogurt

  2 tablespoons Dijon-style mustard
  1 teaspoon freshly ground pepper
  1 hard-cooked egg, chopped
  3 tablespoons minced parsley

In a saucepan, combine shallots, wine, and vinegar. Bring to a boil; boil until reduced by half. Strain and chill. Combine yogurt, mustard, pepper, egg, and parsley. Blend in cooled mixture.

- **Sauce Suzanne**   Omit as in first variation. Substitute:

  1 red onion, quartered
  1 rib celery, sliced
  ½ cup chicken broth
  3 ounces kefir

  1 tablespoon arrowroot flour
  2 tablespoons lemon juice
  Dash nutmeg
  Dash cayenne

Prepare sauce before broiling fillets. Place onion, celery, and water to cover in a saucepan. Bring to a boil; reduce heat. Simmer for 20 minutes; remove from heat; drain. In a blender or food processor, combine chicken broth, kefir, arrowroot, lemon juice, nutmeg, cayenne, and cooked vegetables; blend well. Return to saucepan and heat through.

Salmon and Ginger Cream

Makes 4 servings

Poached salmon is a classic that is superb on its own.
Here, it's enhanced with a smooth ginger cream.

4 salmon steaks
1 cup Gewurztraminer wine or any chablis
1 lemon, thinly sliced
1 onion, thinly sliced
6 whole peppercorns
3 or 4 parsley sprigs

4 ounces Neufchatel cheese, softened
¼ cup plain yogurt
2 teaspoons grated ginger root or
   chopped candied ginger
Grated peel of 1 lemon

Preheat oven to 350° F. Place salmon steaks in an ovenproof baking dish. Pour wine over steaks. Top with lemon, onion, peppercorns, and parsley sprigs. Cover and poach in oven for 15 minutes. In a bowl, combine cheese, yogurt, ginger root, and lemon peel; blend well. Serve at room temperature over hot salmon or serve chilled over cold salmon.

NUTRITIONAL INFORMATION PER SERVING

Calories 395	Saturated Fat 10.2g	Fiber 0.33g	Potassium 646mg
Protein 25.7g	Cholesterol 103mg	Calcium 156mg	Sodium 179mg
Total Fat 24.9g	Carbohydrates 7.7g	Iron 1.9mg	

Variation

● **Cool Cucumber Sauce**   Omit ginger cream ingredients. Substitute:

1 cucumber, peeled, seeded, and grated
4 ounces Neufchatel cheese, softened
2 tablespoons plain yogurt

1 tablespoon lemon juice
1 teaspoon minced dillweed, optional
Salt and white pepper to taste

In a bowl, combine all ingredients; blend well. Serve with salmon steaks.

VEGETARIAN
MEALS

Mexicali Casserole

Makes 8 servings

2 packages (14.5 ounces each) tofu
1 can (28 ounces) no-salt red chili sauce
2 tablespoons chili powder
2 cans (8 ounces each) low-salt tomato sauce
2 tablespoons flour
1 to 2 cloves garlic, minced or pressed
½ teaspoon freshly ground pepper

18 corn tortillas
1 cup shredded Cheddar cheese
8 ounces farmer's cheese, shredded
1 cup diced green peppers
1 cup chopped green onions
¼ cup sliced ripe olives

Drain tofu and freeze for 48 hours. Thaw and wrap tightly in cheesecloth, pressing to squeeze out liquid. Crumble. In a large saucepan, combine red chili sauce, chili powder, and tomato sauces. Blend in flour. Add crumbled tofu, garlic, and pepper. Cook over medium heat, stirring occasionally until heated through. Line the bottom of a 13 x 9-inch baking dish with 6 tortillas. Spread with some of the sauce. Sprinkle with a third of the cheeses, green peppers, and onions. Repeat 2 more times. Top with olives. Bake at 350° F. for 45 minutes or until bubbly and hot.

NUTRITIONAL INFORMATION PER SERVING

Calories 465	Saturated Fat 6.7g	Fiber 2.61g	Potassium 1073mg
Protein 23.4g	Cholesterol 31mg	Calcium 587mg	Sodium 482mg
Total Fat 16.3g	Carbohydrates 61.3g	Iron 5.8mg	

Mexicali Casserole, this page

Brown and Wild Rice Loaf

Makes 4 servings

This dish lends itself well to countless variations and additions. Try sliced mushrooms, nuts, zucchini, crookneck squash, broccoli, cauliflower, or minced leeks.

3 eggs
1½ cups cooked mixed brown and wild rice
2 cups shredded Cheddar cheese
1 cup soft bread crumbs
1 to 2 cloves garlic, minced or pressed

¼ cup diced green pepper
¼ cup chopped red onion
¼ teaspoon salt
2 cups nonfat milk
1 tablespoon butter, melted

In a large bowl, beat eggs. Add remaining ingredients; blend well. Pour into a 1-quart baking dish coated with nonstick vegetable spray. Bake at 325° F. for 45 minutes.

NUTRITIONAL INFORMATION PER SERVING

Calories	455	Saturated Fat	13.1g	Fiber	0.40g	Potassium	363mg
Protein	26.1g	Cholesterol	270mg	Calcium	586mg	Sodium	733mg
Total Fat	25.8g	Carbohydrates	31.3g	Iron	2.2mg		

Barley and Mushroom Casserole

Makes 6 servings

2 red onions, finely chopped
¼ cup water
3 cloves garlic, minced
1 green or red pepper, diced
1 carrot, grated
1 rib celery, sliced
1 pound mushrooms, thinly sliced

1 tablespoon chopped fresh basil or
  1½ teaspoons dried basil leaves
1 cup pearl barley, washed and drained
1½ cups Vegetable Broth or Chicken Broth
  (recipes on pages 114 and 121)
¼ teaspoon freshly ground pepper
3 tablespoons chopped fresh parsley

Preheat oven to 325° F. In an ovenproof Dutch oven, combine onions and water. Cook over medium heat until onions are tender. Add garlic, green pepper, carrot, celery, mushrooms, and basil; simmer gently for 5 minutes. Stir in barley, broth, and pepper. Bring to a boil, stir and remove from heat. Cover and bake for 45 minutes. Sprinkle with parsley and serve.

NUTRITIONAL INFORMATION PER SERVING

Calories	164	Saturated Fat	0.0g	Fiber	1.46g	Potassium	513mg
Protein	6.1g	Cholesterol	0mg	Calcium	39mg	Sodium	28mg
Total Fat	1.0g	Carbohydrates	39.3g	Iron	2.0mg		

Cheese Enchiladas

Makes 4 servings

That Mexican food is not greasy, fattening, or excessively spicy is evidenced by this colorful classic.

¾ cup shredded farmer's cheese
1 can (7 ounces) diced green chilies, drained
1 can (11 ounces) enchilada sauce
⅓ cup chopped red or yellow onion
½ cup plain yogurt

½ cup Neufchatel cheese, softened
1½ cups low-fat cottage cheese
¼ cup hot salsa
8 corn tortillas
¼ cup hot or mild salsa

Set aside ⅓ of the farmer's cheese and chilies for garnish. Cover the bottom of a 12 x 8-inch baking dish with half of the enchilada sauce. In a blender or food processor, combine onion, yogurt, Neufchatel, cottage cheese, and salsa; blend well. Moisten a tortilla with water and heat on both sides in a hot, ungreased skillet until the tortilla is soft and pliable. Place 2 to 3 tablespoons cheese mixture on tortilla; roll up and place seam side down in baking dish. Repeat with remaining tortillas. Cover with remaining enchilada sauce and ¼ cup salsa. Top with any remaining cheese mixture and reserved farmer's cheese and chilies. Cover and bake at 450° F. for 15 minutes or 350° F. for 30 minutes.

NUTRITIONAL INFORMATION PER SERVING

Calories 458	Saturated Fat 8.1g	Fiber 2.23g	Potassium 503mg
Protein 28.5g	Cholesterol 42mg	Calcium 423mg	Sodium 899mg
Total Fat 17.2g	Carbohydrates 47.8g	Iron 5.1mg	

Variation

- **Additional Garnishes**   Sliced ripe olives, minced green onions, sour half-and-half, sliced radishes, cilantro sprigs, sliced yellow wax chilies.

Stir-Fry Pasta Primavera

Makes 4 servings

½ cup unsalted butter
1 medium onion, minced
2 large cloves garlic, pressed or minced
1 pound thin asparagus, cut diagonally in
   ¼-inch slices, tips intact
½ pound mushrooms, thinly sliced
½ pound cauliflower, broken in flowerets
1 zucchini squash, cut in ¼-inch slices
1 small carrot, halved lengthwise
   and cut diagonally in ⅛-inch slices
½ cup Vegetable Broth (recipe on page 114)

¼ cup dry white wine
2 tablespoons chopped fresh basil or
   1 teaspoon dried basil leaves
½ teaspoon oregano leaves
1 cup frozen early peas, thawed
5 green onions, chopped
2 to 3 tablespoons minced parsley or cilantro
   Salt and freshly ground pepper to taste
1 pound linguine or fettucini,
   cooked and drained
½ cup grated Parmesan cheese

Heat a wok or large, deep skillet over medium-high heat. Add butter, onion, and garlic; stir-fry until onion is tender, about 2 minutes. Stir in asparagus, mushrooms, cauliflower, zucchini, and carrot; stir-fry 2 minutes. Increase heat to high. Add broth, wine, basil, and oregano. Bring to a boil; boil until liquid is slightly reduced, about 3 minutes. Add peas and green onions; heat through, stirring gently, for 1 minute. Add parsley, salt, and pepper. Add pasta and cheese; toss until cheese is evenly distributed and pasta is heated through.

NUTRITIONAL INFORMATION PER SERVING

Calories	516	Saturated Fat	16.7g	Fiber	3.53g	Potassium	865mg
Protein	17.6g	Cholesterol	106mg	Calcium	248mg	Sodium	382mg
Total Fat	28.7g	Carbohydrates	52.9g	Iron	4.3mg		

Chickpeas with Herbs

Makes 6 servings

1½ pounds dried chickpeas, soaked
   overnight and drained
1 onion, studded with 4 cloves
1 carrot, minced
2 cloves garlic, minced

Bouquet garni (1 bay leaf, ½ teaspoon
   crushed thyme, 4 sprigs parsley)
½ teaspoon freshly ground black pepper
Juice of ½ lemon
¼ cup minced fresh parsley

In a large kettle, place the first six ingredients with water to cover. Bring to a boil; simmer until chickpeas are tender, about 1 hour. Remove onion and bouquet garni. Drain chickpeas. Sprinkle with lemon juice and parsley. Toss to mix.

NUTRITIONAL INFORMATION PER SERVING

Calories	423	Saturated Fat	0g	Fiber	6.03g	Potassium	994mg
Protein	28.3g	Cholesterol	0mg	Calcium	190mg	Sodium	38mg
Total Fat	5.6g	Carbohydrates	75.4g	Iron	8.4mg		

Stir-Fry Pasta Primavera, this page

Vegetable Patties

Makes 4 servings

1 teaspoon safflower oil
¼ cup diced green onions
6 ounces tempeh (fermented soy bean cake), crumbled
1 clove garlic, minced
1 large carrot, peeled and grated
2 ounces fresh green beans, grated
1 medium rib celery, grated

3 tablespoons plain dried whole-grain bread crumbs, divided
1 egg
1½ teaspoons Worcestershire sauce
⅛ teaspoon freshly ground pepper
2 teaspoons safflower oil
Mustard Sauce

In a skillet, heat 1 teaspoon oil. Sauté green onions for 2 minutes. Add tempeh and garlic. Sauté until lightly browned; set aside. In a bowl, combine carrot and green beans. Place celery in a sieve. Use the back of a spoon to squeeze out liquid. Add celery to carrots and beans. Add 2 tablespoons bread crumbs, egg, Worcestershire, and pepper; blend well. Shape into 4 patties. Sprinkle both sides of patties with remaining 1 tablespoon bread crumbs. Chill 30 minutes. Heat 2 teaspoons oil in skillet. Sauté patties until browned on both sides, turning once. Serve with Mustard Sauce.

NUTRITIONAL INFORMATION PER SERVING

Calories 157	Saturated Fat 0.7g	Fiber 0.94g	Potassium 264mg
Protein 10.5g	Cholesterol 69mg	Calcium 83mg	Sodium 213mg
Total Fat 8.4g	Carbohydrates 12.2g	Iron 1.7mg	

Mustard Sauce

2 tablespoons Dijon-style mustard
2 teaspoons prepared horseradish

2 teaspoons chili sauce
1 teaspoon lemon juice

In a small bowl, combine all ingredients. Cover and chill for at least 1 hour before serving.

Greek Pasta

Makes 8 servings

2 chayotes, peeled, halved, and sliced
2 yellow crookneck squash, sliced
2 zucchini squash, sliced
½ pound mushrooms, sliced
1 or 2 leeks, halved lengthwise, cleaned
   and sliced; or 1 bunch green onions, sliced
4 large tomatoes, coarsely chopped, or
   1 can (28 ounces) Italian-style plum tomatoes
2 to 3 teaspoons lemon juice
1 bay leaf

1 teaspoon basil leaves
1 teaspoon thyme leaves
1 teaspoon oregano leaves
½ teaspoon cinnamon
½ teaspoon rosemary leaves
¼ teaspoon nutmeg
   Freshly cooked pasta, rice, or spaghetti
   squash
   Grated Romano or Parmesan cheese

In a large saucepan, combine all ingredients except the cooked pasta and Romano cheese. Bring to a boil; reduce heat. Cover and simmer for 30 minutes, stirring occasionally. Serve over pasta; top with cheese.

NUTRITIONAL INFORMATION PER SERVING

Calories 86	Saturated Fat 0.0g	Fiber 2.35g	Potassium 789mg	
Protein 4.5g	Cholesterol 1mg	Calcium 88mg	Sodium 14mg	
Total Fat 0.7g	Carbohydrates 18.7g	Iron 2.4mg		

Great Northern Beans

Makes 6 servings

1 pound dried Great Northern beans
2 large red onions, finely chopped
2 to 3 cloves garlic, minced
1 red or green pepper, sliced

1 can (28 ounces) Italian plum tomatoes
½ teaspoon each thyme and oregano
1 teaspoon freshly ground black pepper
¼ cup chopped fresh parsley

In a kettle or large saucepan, place beans with water to cover; bring to a boil. Boil 2 minutes. Cover and let stand 1 hour. Simmer until tender, about 1½ hours; drain. In a skillet, braise onions and garlic in 3 tablespoons water until onions are tender. Add red pepper, tomatoes, thyme, and oregano. Cook 5 minutes, stirring occasionally. Pour beans into serving dish and top with tomato sauce. Garnish with parsley.

NUTRITIONAL INFORMATION PER SERVING

Calories 306	Saturated Fat 0g	Fiber 4.28g	Potassium 1282mg	
Protein 19.1g	Cholesterol 0mg	Calcium 136mg	Sodium 201mg	
Total Fat 1.6g	Carbohydrates 60.2g	Iron 7.1mg		

Vegetables

AND SIDE DISHES

Cauliflower in Lemon Sauce

Makes 6 servings

1 medium head cauliflower
1½ cups water
½ cup nonfat dry milk
1 tablespoon butter

2 cloves garlic, minced or pressed
2 tablespoons chopped parsley
1 tablespoon lemon juice
Tomato slices

Cut off tough end of cauliflower stem and remove outside leaves. Stand cauliflower in a large saucepan. Add water and dry milk. (The milk will prevent discoloration.) Bring to a boil. Reduce heat and simmer, partially covered, just until the stem is tender, 15 minutes. Drain cauliflower; place in a serving dish. In a small saucepan, melt butter. Add garlic, parsley, and lemon juice; blend well. Pour sauce over cauliflower. Arrange overlapping slices of tomato around cauliflower for a nosegay effect.

NUTRITIONAL INFORMATION PER SERVING

Calories 103	Saturated Fat 1.2g	Fiber 1.95g	Potassium 654mg
Protein 8.2g	Cholesterol 7mg	Calcium 169mg	Sodium 89mg
Total Fat 2.4g	Carbohydrates 17.4g	Iron 1.4mg	

Rice Ring with Vegetables, 88;
Overleaf: Cauliflower in Lemon Sauce, this page

Artichoke Sunflower

Makes 4 servings

2 large artichokes, cleaned, trimmed, and cooked
4 ounces Neufchatel cheese, softened
½ teaspoon garlic powder
½ teaspoon onion powder

½ teaspoon hot pepper sauce
1 to 2 tablespoons skim milk
¼ pound cooked small shrimp
Paprika

Remove all leaves from artichokes. Set aside those that are firm enough to handle and have a good edible portion. Cut artichoke hearts into quarters. In a bowl, blend cheese, garlic and onion powders, hot pepper sauce, and enough milk to make a smooth paste. Taste and adjust seasoning. Spread cheese mixture on top of each reserved leaf. Place a small shrimp on top of cheese; dust with paprika. Arrange leaves in concentric circles on a round tray to resemble an open sunflower. Place cut artichoke hearts in center of tray.

NUTRITIONAL INFORMATION PER SERVING

Calories 127	Saturated Fat 4.2g	Fiber 1.43g	Potassium 263mg
Protein 11.6g	Cholesterol 58mg	Calcium 93mg	Sodium 134mg
Total Fat 7.1g	Carbohydrates 7.7g	Iron 1.6mg	

Oriental Asparagus

Makes 6 servings

This dressing is also tasty on cold cooked artichokes.

1½ pounds fresh asparagus, ends trimmed
2 tablespoons lemon juice
2 tablespoons sesame oil
2 tablespoons white wine vinegar

1 to 2 tablespoons chopped watercress or cilantro
2 tablespoons chopped chives
1 to 2 teaspoons minced ginger root

Fill a large saucepan or skillet half full with water. Bring to a boil. Plunge asparagus into boiling water; cook 2 to 4 minutes or until just tender. Drain and chill. In a bowl, combine remaining ingredients; blend well. Pour over asparagus. Chill well before serving.

NUTRITIONAL INFORMATION PER SERVING

Calories 67	Saturated Fat 0.6g	Fiber 0.85g	Potassium 234mg
Protein 2.6g	Cholesterol 0mg	Calcium 26mg	Sodium 1mg
Total Fat 4.8g	Carbohydrates 5.2g	Iron 0.9mg	

Braised Cabbage with Caraway

Makes 6 servings

1 head cabbage (about 1½ pounds), cored
1 teaspoon butter
1 tablespoon minced parsley
1 teaspoon fructose or sugar

½ teaspoon freshly ground pepper
½ cup Chicken Broth (recipe on page 121)
Salt to taste
Caraway seed

Cut cabbage into 6 wedges. In a large skillet, melt butter. Add cabbage, parsley, fructose, pepper, and broth. Cover and cook over medium heat about 12 minutes, basting several times with pan juices. About 1 minute before cabbage is done, sprinkle with salt and caraway seed. Place cabbage in a serving dish. Pour pan liquid over cabbage and serve.

NUTRITIONAL INFORMATION PER SERVING

Calories	35	Saturated Fat	0.5g	Fiber	0.97g	Potassium	187mg
Protein	1.7g	Cholesterol	2mg	Calcium	52mg	Sodium	25mg
Total Fat	1.1g	Carbohydrates	5.6g	Iron	0.7mg		

Braised Carrots Orangerie

Makes 6 servings

12 carrots, peeled and thinly sliced
4 scallions or green onions, sliced
1 teaspoon minced ginger root
2 tablespoons orange juice concentrate
1 tablespoon water

½ cup yogurt
½ cup Neufchatel cheese
¼ teaspoon freshly ground pepper
Grated peel of 1 orange

In a large saucepan, combine carrots, scallions, ginger root, orange juice concentrate, and water. Cover and cook gently for 15 minutes. Stir in yogurt, cheese, and pepper; heat through. Sprinkle with grated orange peel and serve.

NUTRITIONAL INFORMATION PER SERVING

Calories	133	Saturated Fat	3.2g	Fiber	1.76g	Potassium	525mg
Protein	4.7g	Cholesterol	17mg	Calcium	113mg	Sodium	136mg
Total Fat	5.5g	Carbohydrates	18.9g	Iron	1.3mg		

Rice Ring with Vegetables

Makes 4 servings

¼ cup chopped parsley
2 cups hot cooked brown rice
1 tablespoon butter or margarine
2 ribs celery, sliced

1 red pepper, cut in 2-inch julienne strips
¼ cup minced red onion
1½ cups sliced mushrooms
Lemon Sauce

Stir parsley through rice; press rice into a lightly oiled 9-inch ring mold. Invert mold onto a serving plate; keep warm. In a small saucepan, melt butter. Sauté celery, red pepper, onion, and mushrooms over medium-high heat about 5 minutes, stirring often, until vegetables are tender. Spoon vegetable mixture into center of rice ring. Pour Lemon Sauce over top.

Lemon Sauce

½ cup Neufchatel cheese
1 tablespoon plain yogurt
1 tablespoon lemon juice

Pinch saffron powder
2 tablespoons skim milk or Vegetable
Broth (recipe on page 114)

In a small saucepan, combine all ingredients. Cook over low heat, stirring often, until the mixture has the consistency of a medium white sauce.

NUTRITIONAL INFORMATION PER SERVING

Calories 243	Saturated Fat 6.1g	Fiber 0.97g	Potassium 323mg	
Protein 7.1g	Cholesterol 30mg	Calcium 69mg	Sodium 172mg	
Total Fat 10.4g	Carbohydrates 30.8g	Iron 1.2mg		

Spinach Ricotta Balls

Makes 4 servings

1 pound spinach, washed, stemmed, chopped,
  and squeezed dry
½ pound ricotta cheese
2 tablespoons grated Parmesan cheese

¼ teaspoon salt
2 egg yolks
2 tablespoons flour

In a bowl, combine spinach, cheeses, salt, and egg yolks; blend well. Shape into small balls. Dust lightly with flour. Fill a 4-quart saucepan half full with water. Bring to a boil; reduce heat. Drop spinach balls into simmering water. After balls rise to the surface, cook 4 minutes. Remove from water with a slotted spoon.

NUTRITIONAL INFORMATION PER SERVING

Calories 185	Saturated Fat 6.0g	Fiber 0.67g	Potassium 463mg	
Protein 12.8g	Cholesterol 167mg	Calcium 278mg	Sodium 292mg	
Total Fat 11.3g	Carbohydrates 9.4g	Iron 3.5mg		

Braised Chestnuts and Brussels Sprouts

Makes 6 servings

¼ pound mushrooms, sliced
1 tablespoon water
2 tablespoons tomato paste
1 tablespoon cornstarch
2 tablespoons cold water
2 cups Vegetable Broth (recipe on page 114)

1 bouquet garni (½ bay leaf, 4 sprigs parsley, ¼ teaspoon thyme leaves)
1 pound chestnuts, peeled
1 pound brussels sprouts, outer leaves trimmed
1 tablespoon lemon juice
3 tablespoons water
¼ teaspoon freshly ground pepper
¼ teaspoon nutmeg

Place mushrooms and water in a large skillet. Cover; simmer until softened. Stir in tomato paste. Dissolve cornstarch in 2 tablespoons cold water. Stir cornstarch mixture into broth. Add broth mixture, bouquet garni, and chestnuts to mushrooms. Transfer mushroom mixture to casserole; place in the oven. Bake uncovered at 325° F. for 45 minutes. While chestnuts are baking, trim stem end of sprouts and notch with an "x" to speed cooking and eliminate cooking odors. Fill a large saucepan with enough water to cover the sprouts. Bring to a boil; add sprouts. Cook until not quite tender, 5 to 10 minutes. Drain sprouts and place in the skillet. Add lemon juice and 3 tablespoons water. Cook just until tender, about 5 minutes. Remove chestnuts from oven. Discard bouquet garni. Add sprouts to chestnuts. Sprinkle with pepper and nutmeg.

NUTRITIONAL INFORMATION PER SERVING

Calories	170	Saturated Fat	0.0g	Fiber	2.12g	Potassium	630mg
Protein	6.2g	Cholesterol	0mg	Calcium	49mg	Sodium	17mg
Total Fat	1.6g	Carbohydrates	35.5g	Iron	2.6mg		

Spaghetti Squash

Makes 6 servings

1 medium spaghetti squash (2½ pounds)
2 tablespoons butter

Freshly ground pepper to taste

Pierce the squash in several places with the tines of a fork. Place the squash in a large saucepan and cover with cold water. Bring to a boil; cook for 30 minutes or until tender. Cut squash crosswise in half; drain. Using a heavy metal spoon, scrape the spaghetti-like strands into a bowl. Add butter and pepper; toss lightly and serve.

NUTRITIONAL INFORMATION PER SERVING

Calories	139	Saturated Fat	2.4g	Fiber	3.02g	Potassium	772mg
Protein	3.1g	Cholesterol	10mg	Calcium	49mg	Sodium	41mg
Total Fat	4.5g	Carbohydrates	25.8g	Iron	1.4mg		

Lettuce and Vegetable Mélange

Makes 4 servings

1 teaspoon safflower oil
1 medium carrot, peeled and diced
4 large mushrooms, trimmed and diced
4 to 6 green onions, sliced
1½ cups shelled young green peas or 1 package
   (10 ounces) frozen early peas, thawed

2 cups packed shredded lettuce
¼ cup Chicken Broth (recipe on page 121)
1 to 2 teaspoons lemon juice
Nutmeg

In a large skillet, heat oil. Add carrot; cover and cook over medium heat for 3 minutes. Add mushrooms and onions. Cover and cook for 3 minutes. Add peas, lettuce, broth, and lemon juice. Cook, uncovered, until lettuce wilts, tossing occasionally. Sprinkle with nutmeg and serve.

NUTRITIONAL INFORMATION PER SERVING

Calories 91	Saturated Fat 0.1g	Fiber 2.11g	Potassium 324mg
Protein 4.6g	Cholesterol 0mg	Calcium 39mg	Sodium 170mg
Total Fat 1.7g	Carbohydrates 15.4g	Iron 2.1mg	

Green Beans Mexicali

Makes 6 servings

1½ pounds green beans
1 tablespoon butter
1 red onion, thinly sliced
5 tablespoons water
3 cloves garlic, minced
½ teaspoon turmeric

2 to 3 tablespoons hot salsa
¼ teaspoon cumin
2 teaspoons lemon or lime juice
2 teaspoons chopped cilantro
Fresh coriander, optional

Wash, trim, and slice beans diagonally into 1-inch lengths. In a large skillet over medium-high heat, melt butter. Add beans, onion, and water; stir. Cover and steam until tender, about 7 minutes. Add remaining ingredients. Season to taste.

NUTRITIONAL INFORMATION PER SERVING

Calories 55	Saturated Fat 1.2g	Fiber 1.36g	Potassium 224mg
Protein 2.3g	Cholesterol 5mg	Calcium 67mg	Sodium 27mg
Total Fat 2.3g	Carbohydrates 12.5g	Iron 1.0mg	

Lettuce Mélange, this page

Fettucini Alfredo

Makes 4 servings

Here's a classic favorite adapted to suit a healthier life-style.

2 quarts Chicken Broth (recipe on page 121)
1 pound fresh fettucini
1 package (8 ounces) Neufchatel cheese, softened
½ cup plain yogurt
1 tablespoon butter

2 or 3 cloves garlic, minced or pressed
¼ cup minced parsley
¼ cup grated Parmesan cheese
   Freshly ground nutmeg, white pepper, and/or poppy seed

In a large saucepan, bring broth to a boil. Add fettucini; cook until tender-firm, 4 to 6 minutes. Drain pasta, reserving broth for other uses; set aside. In a small bowl, blend cheese and yogurt until smooth; set aside. In a large skillet, melt butter. Sauté garlic 1 minute. Reduce heat to low. Add yogurt-cheese mixture; blend well. Add pasta. Sprinkle with parsley and Parmesan cheese; toss lightly. Garnish with nutmeg, white pepper, or poppy seed.

NUTRITIONAL INFORMATION PER SERVING

Calories 715	Saturated Fat 12.7g	Fiber 3.84g	Potassium 805mg
Protein 31.7g	Cholesterol 62mg	Calcium 210mg	Sodium 524mg
Total Fat 23.0g	Carbohydrates 97.2g	Iron 4.8mg	

Colorful Couscous

Makes 4 servings

3 cups Chicken Broth (recipe on page 121)
2 cups couscous
½ cup thinly sliced mushrooms

¼ cup pine nuts or sliced almonds, toasted
¼ cup minced parsley
¼ cup minced red onion

In a medium saucepan, bring broth to a boil. Stir in remaining ingredients. Immediately remove from heat. Cover and let stand until liquid is absorbed, about 5 minutes. Fluff with a fork before serving.

NUTRITIONAL INFORMATION PER SERVING

Calories 371	Saturated Fat 0.3g	Fiber 0.39g	Potassium 342mg
Protein 15.4g	Cholesterol 1mg	Calcium 47mg	Sodium 64mg
Total Fat 5.6g	Carbohydrates 63.7g	Iron 2.6mg	

Corn Bread Stuffing

Makes 8 servings

This stuffing is excellent served with Baked Chops with Apples and Onions (page 56). Omit apples from the Baked Chops recipe. Place stuffing in the bottom of the baking dish before topping with remaining ingredients.

2 packages (6 ounces each) corn bread stuffing
½ cup safflower oil
1 Golden Delicious apple, cored and diced
1 Red Delicious apple, cored and diced
1 package (3½ ounces) whole almonds
2 ribs celery, sliced

1 medium red onion, peeled and diced
½ cup minced parsley
¼ cup sunflower seed
¼ cup wheat germ
1½ cups orange or apple juice

In a large bowl, combine stuffing mix and oil; toss lightly. Add apples, almonds, celery, onion, parsley, sunflower seed, and wheat germ; mix lightly. Pour in orange juice; blend gently but thoroughly. Turn into a lightly oiled 2-quart mold. Bake at 350° F. for 35 minutes.

NUTRITIONAL INFORMATION PER SERVING

Calories	534	Saturated Fat	2.0g	Fiber	1.03g	Potassium	352mg
Protein	11.0g	Cholesterol	0mg	Calcium	86mg	Sodium	9mg
Total Fat	35.1g	Carbohydrates	46.2g	Iron	4.3mg		

Savory Bulgur Pilaf

Makes 4 servings

1 tablespoon butter
¼ cup minced onion
¼ cup chopped green pepper
1 or 2 cloves garlic, minced
3 cups water

1 cup white wine
2 cups bulgur
2 cups sliced mushrooms
2 or 3 tablespoons minced parsley

In a medium saucepan, melt butter over medium-high heat. Sauté onion, green pepper, and garlic until tender. Stir in remaining ingredients. Cover and bring to a boil; reduce heat. Simmer 15 minutes. Fluff with a fork before serving.

NUTRITIONAL INFORMATION PER SERVING

Calories	404	Saturated Fat	1.8g	Fiber	1.95g	Potassium	481mg
Protein	9.1g	Cholesterol	8mg	Calcium	42mg	Sodium	42mg
Total Fat	4.3g	Carbohydrates	77.9g	Iron	5.0mg		

BREADS
AND SANDWICHES

Whole Wheat Irish Soda Bread
Makes 2 loaves (16 servings)

2 cups all-purpose flour
2 cups whole wheat flour
2 teaspoons salt
1¼ teaspoons baking soda (1 teaspoon
if using buttermilk)

¼ teaspoon ground cardamom or coriander
½ cup water
1¼ cups yogurt
1 egg, lightly beaten
1 cup currants or raisins, optional

Preheat oven to 375° F. In a large mixing bowl, combine dry ingredients. In a separate bowl, stir water into yogurt. Blend in egg. Stir liquids into dry ingredients; blend well. Turn dough out onto a lightly floured surface. Knead 3 to 4 minutes or until dough is smooth. Divide dough in half. Shape each half into an 8-inch round. Place dough rounds in 2 buttered 8-inch round baking pans. Press to edges of pans. Make a criss-cross slash about ½ inch deep into the top of each loaf. Bake for 35 to 40 minutes or until golden brown. To serve, cut into wedges, split, and butter.

NUTRITIONAL INFORMATION PER LOAF

Calories	144	Saturated Fat	0.6g	Fiber	0.6g	Potassium	173mg
Protein	5.8g	Cholesterol	21mg	Calcium	69mg	Sodium	322mg
Total Fat	1.7g	Carbohydrates	26.9g	Iron	1.1mg		

Ethnic Pita Sandwiches (variation: Curry Shrimp), 102

Savory Muffins

Makes 8 servings

Make muffins ahead on the weekend for lunches or a quick breakfast snack.

1 egg
1 cup skim milk
3 to 4 tablespoons safflower oil or butter
1 cup all-purpose flour
1 cup whole wheat flour

3 tablespoons brown sugar
2 tablespoons wheat germ
2 teaspoons baking powder
½ teaspoon salt
½ teaspoon baking soda

Preheat oven to 400° F. Grease bottoms only of 12 muffin cups. In a bowl, beat egg, milk, and oil. Stir together remaining ingredients; add to liquid mixture all at once. Mix just until dry ingredients are moistened. Batter will be lumpy. Fill muffin cups ⅔ full with batter. Bake 20 to 25 minutes or until golden brown. Turn out of pan immediately.

NUTRITIONAL INFORMATION PER SERVING

Calories 205	Saturated Fat 0.8g	Fiber 0.40g	Potassium 185mg
Protein 6.0g	Cholesterol 35mg	Calcium 55mg	Sodium 266mg
Total Fat 7.3g	Carbohydrates 29.4g	Iron 1.4mg	

Variations

- **Cereal Muffins**   Decrease milk to ½ cup. Omit whole wheat flour. Add 2 cups whole wheat flakes, cornflakes, or oatmeal to batter.
- **Peanut Butter and Jelly Muffins**   Fill muffin cups half full with batter. Drop 1 teaspoon peanut butter and 1 teaspoon jelly into centers of each. Add batter until cups are two-thirds full.
- **Sweet Fruit Muffins**   Stir in 1 cup blueberries or cranberries and 1 tablespoon grated lemon peel.
- **Apple Spice Muffins**   Stir in 1 cup grated apple and ½ teaspoon cinnamon or pumpkin pie spice.
- **Nut-Topped Muffins**   Combine ⅓ cup brown sugar, ⅓ cup chopped nuts, and ½ teaspoon cinnamon or pumpkin pie spice. Sprinkle over batter in muffin cups.
- **Cornmeal Muffins**   Substitute 1 cup cornmeal for whole wheat flour.

Old-Fashioned Scones

Makes 8 servings

2 cups flour
1 tablespoon baking powder
¼ teaspoon salt
3 tablespoons butter

2 eggs (reserve 1 tablespoon egg white), lightly beaten
⅓ cup evaporated milk
Sugar or grated Parmesan cheese, optional

In a large bowl, stir together dry ingredients. Cut in butter until mixture resembles fine crumbs. Add eggs and evaporated milk; mix until a stiff dough forms. Turn dough out onto a lightly floured board. Knead quickly until dough holds together. Divide dough in half. Pat each half into a circle 6 inches in diameter and 1 inch thick. Cut each circle into quarters. Arrange quarters 1 inch apart on a large baking sheet. Brush tops with reserved egg white. Sprinkle with sugar or grated Parmesan cheese, if desired. Bake at 400° F. for 15 minutes or until golden brown. Scones are best when served hot.

NUTRITIONAL INFORMATION PER SERVING

Calories	206	Saturated Fat	2.7g	Fiber	0.05g	Potassium	127mg
Protein	6.6g	Cholesterol	85mg	Calcium	67mg	Sodium	257mg
Total Fat	5.9g	Carbohydrates	27.6g	Iron	1.3mg		

Variations

- **Cheese Scones**   Add ½ cup shredded Cheddar cheese.
- **Orange Scones**   Add 1 tablespoon grated orange peel and ¼ teaspoon vanilla or 1 teaspoon Cointreau. Frost with powdered sugar and orange juice mixed to a spreading consistency.
- **Whole Wheat and Herb Scones**   Decrease flour to 1⅓ cups. Add ½ cup fresh chopped herbs of your choice. A good combination is chopped parsley, chives, and basil leaves.
- **Raisin and Orange Scones**   Add ½ cup raisins and the grated peel of 1 orange.

Savory Corn Bread

Makes 6 servings

½ cup all-purpose flour
¼ cup whole wheat pastry flour
2½ teaspoons baking powder
 1 to 2 teaspoons brown sugar
½ teaspoon salt

1¼ cups yellow or white stone-ground cornmeal
1 cup skim milk
1 egg, lightly beaten
2 tablespoons butter, melted

Preheat oven to 425° F. Lightly grease 12 muffin cups or a 9-inch square baking pan. Place in oven until hot enough to make a drop of water sizzle. In a bowl, stir together dry ingredients. In a separate bowl, combine milk, egg, and butter; blend well. Add dry ingredients; beat with rapid strokes until blended. Fill hot muffin cups two-thirds full with batter. Bake for 15 minutes or until golden brown.

NUTRITIONAL INFORMATION PER SERVING

Calories 215	Saturated Fat 2.7g	Fiber 0.38g	Potassium 222mg
Protein 6.6g	Cholesterol 57mg	Calcium 66mg	Sodium 341mg
Total Fat 5.9g	Carbohydrates 34.2g	Iron 1.2mg	

Variations

- **Chili Corn Bread**   Add ½ to 1 can (4 ounces) diced green chilies.
- **Cheese Corn Bread**   Add ¼ to ⅓ cup shredded cheese of your choice.
- **Health Corn Bread**   Add ¼ cup wheat germ or ¼ cup additional cornmeal.

Baguettes

Makes 1 loaf

I made these long, crisp loaves of French bread for many catering and restaurant functions, sometimes making as many as thirty loaves at a time. The bread rises quickly and the recipe can be doubled easily. Baguettes take more than sixty minutes to make, but the extra time is well worth spending.

1 package (¼ ounce) active dry yeast
¼ cup lukewarm water (100 to 115° F.)
5 cups all-purpose flour
¼ to ½ cup gluten (bread) flour, optional
1½ tablespoons sugar

2 teaspoons salt
1¾ cups lukewarm water
Cornmeal
1 teaspoon cornstarch
½ cup water

Dissolve yeast in ¼ cup water; let stand 5 minutes. In a large mixing bowl, combine flours, sugar, salt, and 1¾ cups water; mix until well blended. Turn dough out onto a lightly floured surface. Knead for 15 minutes or until dough is smooth and elastic. Place dough in a greased bowl; turn once to grease top. Cover with plastic wrap and place in a warm, draft-free place 1 hour or until doubled in bulk.

Punch dough down and turn out onto a lightly floured surface. Divide into thirds. Shape each third into an 8- to 10-inch roll with tapered ends. Roll each piece back and forth rapidly, beginning at the center and gently pulling from center to ends, until loaf is 18 to 20 inches long. (Length will be determined by the size of baking sheet and size of oven.) Place loaf diagonally across a greased large baking sheet sprinkled with cornmeal. Cover lightly with plastic wrap. Let rise for 15 to 20 minutes or until puffy but *not* doubled in bulk. In a small saucepan, combine cornstarch and ½ cup water. Bring to a boil, stirring often. Remove from heat and cool slightly. Uncover loaf and brush top and sides with cornstarch mixture. With a sharp knife, cut ½-inch-deep diagonal slashes the length of the loaf. Bake in a preheated 375° F. oven for 15 minutes. Brush with cornstarch mixture; bake 10 minutes. Brush again with cornstarch and bake 10 to 15 minutes or until loaf is golden brown and sounds hollow when lightly tapped. Remove from baking sheet to a wire rack to cool. To serve in the French Provincial manner, break the loaf apart at the dinner table or slice into 16 slices.

NUTRITIONAL INFORMATION PER SERVING

Calories 176	Saturated Fat 0.0g	Fiber 0.08g	Potassium 53mg
Protein 6.1g	Cholesterol 0mg	Calcium 10mg	Sodium 268mg
Total Fat 0.5g	Carbohydrates 35.9g	Iron 1.3mg	

Overleaf: (Clockwise from upper right) Baguettes, 99; Savory Corn Bread, 98; Old-Fashioned Scones, 97; Savory Muffins, 96; Whole Wheat Irish Soda Bread, 95

Ethnic Pita Sandwiches

Makes 4 servings

2 pita breads
¼ cup Minceur Mayonnaise (recipe on page 42)
1 tablespoon Dijon-style mustard
¼ cup shredded lettuce or alfalfa sprouts
4 lettuce leaves

4 slices Provolone cheese
4 slices tomato
4 slices cucumber
Fillings: Curry Shrimp, Mediterranean Chicken, or Oriental Turkey

Wrap pita breads in a damp towel and warm in the oven at 350° F. for 10 minutes. Cut pitas in half. Combine mayonnaise and mustard. Spread mayonnaise mixture inside pitas. Line the bottom half of each pita with shredded lettuce. Top with a lettuce leaf and 1 slice each of provolone, tomato, and cucumber. Fill with your choice of filling.

NUTRITIONAL INFORMATION PER SERVING

Calories	268	Saturated Fat	4.9g	Fiber	0.45g	Potassium	215mg
Protein	11.6g	Cholesterol	41mg	Calcium	195mg	Sodium	586mg
Total Fat	13.6g	Carbohydrates	27.0g	Iron	1.7mg		

Curry Shrimp

1 can (4½ ounces) broken shrimp, drained
½ cup chopped green apple
Minceur Mayonnaise (recipe on page 42)

Lemon juice to taste
Curry powder to taste

Gently mix shrimp and apple with enough mayonnaise to bind. Blend in lemon juice and curry powder.

Mediterranean Chicken

1½ to 2 cups chopped cooked chicken
½ cup green pepper strips, sautéed
¼ cup sliced ripe olives

2 to 3 tablespoons tomato paste
½ teaspoon basil leaves
½ teaspoon thyme leaves

Combine all ingredients; blend well. Spoon into pitas and heat through in a 350° F. oven.

Oriental Turkey

1½ to 2 cups shredded cooked turkey
½ cup sliced water chestnuts
½ cup bean sprouts
2 to 3 tablespoons Minceur Mayonnaise (recipe on page 42)

2 to 3 tablespoons plain yogurt
Soy sauce to taste
Ground coriander to taste
Ground ginger to taste

Combine all ingredients; blend well.

Indian-Style Sandwich

Makes 4 servings

4 chapati rounds, toasted corn or flour
   tortillas, or whole wheat pita bread
1 teaspoon safflower oil
1 pound ground turkey
½ cup chopped red onion
½ cup chopped green pepper
½ cup raisins
2 cloves garlic, minced or pressed
½ pound mushrooms, sliced

1 to 3 teaspoons curry powder
¼ teaspoon ground cumin
¼ teaspoon freshly ground pepper
2 cups shredded iceberg lettuce
2 medium tomatoes, sliced
1 avocado, peeled, pitted, and sliced
½ cup grated carrot
¼ cup plain yogurt
   Lime wedges

Place chapatis in a damp towel and warm in the oven at 350° F. for 10 to 15 minutes. In a large skillet, heat oil. Sauté turkey 2 to 3 minutes, breaking up with a fork. Add onion, green pepper, raisins, garlic, mushrooms, curry powder, cumin, and pepper. Cook until turkey is golden, stirring often. Remove from heat. Place chapatis on individual plates. Top with lettuce, turkey mixture, tomatoes, avocado, carrot, and yogurt. Garnish with lime wedges.

NUTRITIONAL INFORMATION PER SERVING

Calories 489	Saturated Fat 3.3g	Fiber 3.78g	Potassium 1456mg
Protein 34.7g	Cholesterol 65mg	Calcium 106mg	Sodium 411mg
Total Fat 17.7g	Carbohydrates 59.1g	Iron 5.4mg	

California BLT

Makes 4 servings

1 ripe avocado
1 tablespoon Minceur Mayonnaise
   (recipe on page 42)
1 teaspoon lemon or lime juice

8 slices whole wheat bread, toasted
8 slices crisp-cooked bacon
8 slices tomato
   Spinach leaves or alfalfa sprouts

In a small bowl, mash avocado. Blend in mayonnaise and lemon juice. Spread avocado mixture over 4 slices toast. Top with a layer of bacon, tomato, and spinach. Top with remaining toast.

NUTRITIONAL INFORMATION PER SERVING

Calories 332	Saturated Fat 3.8g	Fiber 2.51g	Potassium 684mg
Protein 10.4g	Cholesterol 11mg	Calcium 67mg	Sodium 488mg
Total Fat 19.3g	Carbohydrates 33.3g	Iron 3.2mg	

Italian Sausage and Pepper Pitas

Makes 4 servings

2 pita breads
½ pound ground hot Italian sausage
⅓ cup tomato sauce
½ green pepper, diced

½ small onion, chopped
½ teaspoon oregano leaves
½ teaspoon basil leaves
4 eggs, lightly beaten

Wrap pita breads in a damp towel and warm in the oven at 350° F. for 10 minutes. In a large skillet, sauté sausage about 5 minutes or until browned, stirring to break up; drain fat. Stir in tomato sauce, green pepper, onion, oregano, basil, and eggs. Cook, stirring often, until eggs are set. Cut pitas in half. Spoon filling into pita bread halves and serve.

NUTRITIONAL INFORMATION PER SERVING

Calories	354	Saturated Fat	5.4g	Fiber	0.48g	Potassium	293mg
Protein	19.7g	Cholesterol	307mg	Calcium	58mg	Sodium	906mg
Total Fat	18.1g	Carbohydrates	28.8g	Iron	3.2mg		

Quesadillas

Makes 4 servings

2 cups shredded Monterey Jack, Cheddar,
or Swiss cheese, or combination
4 flour tortillas

½ cup diced green chilies
4 to 8 tablespoons Mexican table sauce,
optional

Divide cheese over tortillas, covering one half of each to within ½ inch of the edge. Top with chilies and Mexican table sauce. Fold tortillas in half. Place on a large baking sheet. Bake at 450° F. for 5 minutes or until tortillas are golden brown and cheese melts.

NUTRITIONAL INFORMATION PER SERVING

Calories	326	Saturated Fat	10.4g	Fiber	0.53g	Potassium	79mg
Protein	18.1g	Cholesterol	54mg	Calcium	536mg	Sodium	306mg
Total Fat	18.8g	Carbohydrates	21.5g	Iron	1.7mg		

--- Variations ---

• Reduce cheese to ¼ cup. Add ¼ cup diced cooked sausage, chicken, turkey, beef, or bacon.
• Add sliced green or red onion and chopped avocado to taste.

Calamari Poor Boy

Makes 4 servings

½ cup flour
¼ teaspoon basil leaves
¼ teaspoon oregano leaves
2 tablespoons milk
1 egg, lightly beaten
¼ cup Neufchatel cheese
¼ cup cottage cheese
4 squid steaks (1½ pounds)

½ cup bread crumbs
1 tablespoon butter
1 tablespoon safflower oil
4 French rolls, toasted
½ small red onion, thinly sliced and
   separated into rings
1 grapefruit, segmented
4 lettuce leaves
1 lime, cut in 4 wedges

On a large plate or breadboard, mix flour, basil, and oregano. In a wide, shallow bowl, beat milk and egg together. Blend cheeses; set aside. Dredge steaks in flour mixture, dip into egg mixture, then roll in bread crumbs. In a large skillet, heat butter and oil. Sauté steaks for 30 to 35 seconds on each side, adding more butter as needed. On bottoms of rolls, layer steaks, onion rings, and grapefruit. Spread tops of rolls with blended cheeses. Top with lettuce and garnish with lime wedges.

NUTRITIONAL INFORMATION PER SERVING

Calories 478	Saturated Fat 5.0g	Fiber 0.65g	Potassium 269mg
Protein 39.1g	Cholesterol 90mg	Calcium 98mg	Sodium 370mg
Total Fat 13.7g	Carbohydrates 47.8g	Iron 2.6mg	

Tacos

Makes 12 tacos

1 pound lean ground beef
1 small onion, chopped
½ teaspoon oregano leaves or ground cumin
¼ teaspoon garlic powder
¼ teaspoon salt

12 taco shells or warmed corn tortillas
¼ to ½ cup diced green chilies
1 cup shredded Cheddar cheese
1 cup taco sauce
Shredded iceberg lettuce

In a large skillet, brown ground beef and onion; drain fat. Stir in seasonings. Divide beef mixture among taco shells. Top with chilies, cheese, taco sauce, and lettuce.

NUTRITIONAL INFORMATION PER SERVING

Calories 171	Saturated Fat 3.5g	Fiber 0.62g	Potassium 144mg
Protein 12g	Cholesterol 29.3mg	Calcium 141mg	Sodium 119mg
Total Fat 6.8g	Carbohydrates 15.7g	Iron 2.2mg	

BREAKFAST
AND BRUNCH

Potato Latkes
Makes twelve 3-inch pancakes

In my variation of a classic Jewish recipe, I use grated Parmesan cheese to bind the zucchini and grated potatoes. These pancakes reheat easily and can be carried in an aluminum foil packet to take on the run. Try sandwiching kefir, applesauce, or other fillings between two pancakes.

2 medium baking potatoes, peeled and grated
2 medium zucchini squash, shredded
¼ cup minced green onion
¼ cup grated Parmesan cheese
2 eggs

2 to 3 tablespoons minced parsley
1 tablespoon butter
1 tablespoon safflower oil
Sour half-and-half
Applesauce

Wrap grated potatoes in a clean tea towel or cheesecloth; press to absorb moisture. Stir together potatoes, zucchini, green onion, cheese, eggs, and parsley. In a large skillet, heat butter and oil. Drop pancake batter into the oil by heaping spoonfuls and flatten to 3-inch patties about ¼ inch thick. Fry until crisp and brown on both sides. Serve very hot with sour half-and-half and applesauce. (To keep latkes warm, place on paper towels on a baking sheet in a 200° F. oven.)

NUTRITIONAL INFORMATION PER PANCAKE

Calories 88	Saturated Fat 1.8g	Fiber 0.42g	Potassium 201mg
Protein 2.8g	Cholesterol 52mg	Calcium 44mg	Sodium 57mg
Total Fat 4.4g	Carbohydrates 9.8g	Iron 0.6mg	

Potato Latkes, this page
Overleaf: (Clockwise from upper right) Basque Omelet, 111;
Roquefort Apple Omelet, 112; Classic Omelet
(variation: Taiwan Wok Omelet), 110

Classic Omelet

Makes 1 serving

This is the Cordon Bleu way to make the best and fastest omelet. As you gain confidence, try cooking in two pans at once with the fillings on the side and ready to go!

3 eggs (omit 1 yolk to lower cholesterol,
  if desired)
1 tablespoon water
1 tablespoon butter

1 teaspoon minced fresh parsley
1 teaspoon basil leaves
1 teaspoon minced chives

Heat a 7- or 8-inch omelet pan over medium-high heat. Beat eggs and water with a fork until well blended but not foamy. Add butter to pan. When butter foams, pour in the eggs. Slowly stir counterclockwise three times with a fork. Wait 3 seconds or until outer edge is set. With a fork, draw cooked portion at edge toward center, tilting pan as necessary, so the uncooked portion will reach the hot pan surface. While the top is still moist and creamy, add herbs or filling. With a spatula, fold omelet in half. Shake pan gently to release omelet. Transfer to warm serving plate.

NUTRITIONAL INFORMATION PER SERVING

Calories 281	Saturated Fat 10.4g	Fiber 0.30g	Potassium 244mg
Protein 15.8g	Cholesterol 580mg	Calcium 97mg	Sodium 306mg
Total Fat 22.5g	Carbohydrates 2.7g	Iron 2.7mg	

Variations

- Fill each omelet with 3 to 4 tablespoons of stir-fried Oriental vegetables such as sugar peas, bean sprouts, bok choy, and water chestnuts.
- **Taiwan Wok Omelet**   This may be made in your wok or in an omelet pan. Simply heat a filling of your choice of Oriental or Western vegetables. Any root vegetables may be sliced and sautéed quickly first, such as carrots and onions along with minced garlic and ginger as seasonings. Fry and use fresh sugar peas, bean sprouts, bok choy and water chestnuts. Prepare the omelet as usual and fill; garnish as desired. The egg foo yung sauce makes a fine additional topping. Measurements of each ingredient are not necessary since you know the technique and how to experiment! As a reminder, it's 3 to 4 tablespoons or whatever is needed to fill the omelet fully.

Basque Omelet

Makes 6 servings

The variations on this tomato-based sauce could be endless.
All sauces are superb over scrambled eggs or pasta.

1 teaspoon butter
1 teaspoon olive oil
½ cup chopped green pepper
½ cup chopped red onion
1 cup sliced mushrooms
1 can (16 ounces) whole peeled or
  plum tomatoes, broken up

1 to 2 cloves garlic, minced
¼ teaspoon hot pepper sauce
1 teaspoon cornstarch, optional
1 teaspoon water, optional
  Salt and freshly ground pepper to taste
4 Classic Omelets (recipe on page 110)

In a saucepan, heat butter and oil. Sauté green pepper and onion until tender. Add mushrooms, tomatoes, garlic, and hot pepper sauce. Simmer until mixture is slightly reduced and thickened. If a still thicker sauce is desired, dissolve cornstarch in water and stir into sauce. Bring to a boil; reduce heat. Simmer, stirring constantly, until thickened. Prepare Classic Omelets, adding 3 to 4 tablespoons of the sauce to the center of each before folding over. Spoon a few tablespoons sauce over each omelet and serve.

NUTRITIONAL INFORMATION PER SERVING

Calories	346	Saturated Fat	11.2g	Fiber	1.58g	Potassium	647mg
Protein	18.1g	Cholesterol	583mg	Calcium	115mg	Sodium	605mg
Total Fat	25.0g	Carbohydrates	15.3g	Iron	3.8mg		

Variations

- **Mexican Sauce**   Add diced green chilies, sliced jalapeno or yellow wax chilies, and chili powder to taste.
- **Creole Sauce**   Add chopped onion, 1 whole clove, and ¼ teaspoon marjoram leaves.
- **Italian Sauce**   Add cooked and crumbled hot Italian sausage and minced basil to taste.

Roquefort Apple Omelet

Makes 2 servings

This omelet combines the intense flavor of Roquefort cheese with crisp apple slices. This is a delightfully different dish to try for breakfast or brunch!

1 tablespoon butter
1 tart green apple, cored and thinly sliced
2 to 3 tablespoons grated Parmesan
   or shredded Monterey Jack cheese, optional

1¼ ounces Roquefort or Neufchatel cheese
2 Classic Omelets without herbs
   (recipe on page 110)
Watercress or parsley sprigs

In a saucepan, melt butter. Stir in apple and cheeses. Heat through and keep warm on low heat. Fill each omelet with half of the apple-cheese mixture. Garnish omelets with watercress.

NUTRITIONAL INFORMATION PER SERVING

Calories 466	Saturated Fat 18.5g	Fiber 0.80g	Potassium 348mg
Protein 22.3g	Cholesterol 617mg	Calcium 307mg	Sodium 802mg
Total Fat 35.7g	Carbohydrates 13.7g	Iron 2.9mg	

Basque Eggs

Makes 6 servings

6 hard-cooked eggs, sliced
2 to 3 cups pimiento strips
   Sliced ripe olives
1 tablespoon minced shallots or green onions
1 teaspoon paprika
1 teaspoon Dijon-style mustard

2 tablespoons wine vinegar
¼ cup safflower oil
2 tablespoons water
   Salt, freshly ground pepper,
   and sugar to taste

Arrange egg slices on a serving platter. Arrange pimiento strips over eggs in a lattice pattern. Place an olive slice in each lattice opening. Blend remaining ingredients. Before serving, drizzle dressing over eggs.

NUTRITIONAL INFORMATION PER SERVING

Calories 234	Saturated Fat 2.4g	Fiber 1.21g	Potassium 87mg
Protein 7.3g	Cholesterol 275mg	Calcium 38mg	Sodium 564mg
Total Fat 19.9g	Carbohydrates 8.3g	Iron 2.7mg	

Whole Wheat Health Pancakes

Makes twelve 4-inch pancakes

These are great served with a fruit puree or flavored ricotta spread.
They can also be served with syrup or honey which has been flavored with a
little Grand Marnier and grated orange and lemon peel.

1 cup all-purpose flour
¾ cup whole wheat pastry flour
2 tablespoons cornmeal
2 tablespoons wheat germ
2 tablespoons baking powder
1 teaspoon baking soda

¼ teaspoon salt
2 eggs, lightly beaten
1 cup plain yogurt
1 cup skim milk
2 tablespoons safflower oil

In a mixing bowl, stir together the first seven ingredients. Add remaining ingredients; stir vigorously until smooth. Heat oil in a lightly oiled large skillet over medium-high heat. Cook pancakes by quarter cupfuls until golden brown on both sides.

NUTRITIONAL INFORMATION PER SERVING

Calories 129	Saturated Fat 0.9g	Fiber 0.22g	Potassium 184mg
Protein 5.0g	Cholesterol 49mg	Calcium 60mg	Sodium 254mg
Total Fat 4.3g	Carbohydrates 17.8g	Iron 0.9mg	

Shrimp Foo Yung

Makes 4 servings

4 eggs, lightly beaten
1 cup fresh bean sprouts
5 to 6 green onions, thinly sliced
1 can (6½ ounces) baby shrimp or crab meat

1 clove garlic, minced
1 tablespoon butter
1 tablespoon safflower oil
Foo Yung Sauce

In a mixing bowl, stir together eggs, bean sprouts, green onions, shrimp or crab meat, and garlic. In a large frying pan, heat butter and oil over medium-high heat. Form patties by ladling ¼ cupfuls of egg mixture into hot butter. Sauté until browned on both sides. Add more oil as necessary. Serve topped with Foo Yung Sauce.

Foo Yung Sauce

1 teaspoon cornstarch
1 teaspoon sugar
1 teaspoon vinegar

½ teaspoon grated ginger root
2 teaspoons soy sauce
½ cup Chicken Broth (recipe on page 121)

In a small saucepan, combine all ingredients. Heat and stir until thickened.

NUTRITIONAL INFORMATION PER SERVING

Calories 225	Saturated Fat 3.8g	Fiber 0.69g	Potassium 302mg
Protein 19.6g	Cholesterol 339mg	Calcium 109mg	Sodium 283mg
Total Fat 12.7g	Carbohydrates 10.0g	Iron 3.3mg	

WEEKEND
COOKING

Vegetable Broth
Makes 3 quarts (12 servings)

*This has none of the fat, salt, or MSG found in canned broth.
It does have all of the delicacy of fresh vegetables.*

1 tablespoon safflower oil
2 onions, peeled and thickly sliced
2 ribs celery, sliced
3 large carrots, scrubbed and coarsely chopped
1 turnip, scrubbed and roughly chopped
1 potato, scrubbed and coarsely chopped

3 quarts water
2 to 3 cloves garlic
6 parsley sprigs
½ bay leaf
1 teaspoon thyme leaves

In a large saucepan or kettle, heat oil. Sauté vegetables until tender, about 8 to 10 minutes. Add water and seasonings. Bring to a boil; reduce heat. Cover and simmer for 1 to 1½ hours. Strain through a sieve to remove vegetables and seasonings. Use in any recipe calling for vegetable broth, as a soup base, and to thin sauces. Can be frozen in ice cube trays for ready use.

NUTRITIONAL INFORMATION PER SERVING

Calories 16	Saturated Fat 0.0g	Fiber 0.00g	Potassium 0mg
Protein 1.3g	Cholesterol 0mg	Calcium 0mg	Sodium 0mg
Total Fat 0.6g	Carbohydrates 2.6g	Iron 0.4mg	

Veal Ragout, 117

Continental Turkey with Water Chestnuts

Makes 4 servings

¼ cup safflower oil
1 bunch green onions, diagonally sliced
1 rib celery, diagonally sliced
1 red or green pepper, sliced
2 tablespoons toasted slivered almonds
1 can (8 ounces) water chestnuts,
    drained and thinly sliced
3 cups diced cooked turkey or chicken
2 tablespoons flour

2 tablespoons paprika
2 to 3 teaspoons curry powder
½ to 1 teaspoon basil leaves
1¾ cups Chicken or Beef Broth (recipes
    on page 121)
2 tablespoons chopped pimiento
    Salt and freshly ground pepper to taste
    Fluffy hot rice

In a large skillet, heat oil. Sauté green onions, celery, and red pepper until vegetables are tender. Add almonds, water chestnuts, and turkey; mix lightly. Stir in flour, paprika, curry powder, and basil. Sauté lightly, stirring constantly. Stir in broth and pimiento. Cover and steam briefly. Season with salt and pepper. Serve with rice.

NUTRITIONAL INFORMATION PER SERVING

Calories 426	Saturated Fat 3.4g	Fiber 2.11g	Potassium 841mg
Protein 22.3g	Cholesterol 87mg	Calcium 77mg	Sodium 195mg
Total Fat 22.9g	Carbohydrates 19.5g	Iron 4.4mg	

Variations

- **Oriental Turkey**   Omit flour, paprika, curry powder, and basil. Decrease chicken broth to 1 cup. Add:

2 tablespoons cornstarch
¼ teaspoon garlic powder
1 teaspoon grated ginger root or
    ¼ teaspoon ground ginger

¼ cup low-salt soy sauce
2 tablespoons dry sherry
    Freshly ground pepper to taste

Stir cornstarch, garlic powder, and ginger root into turkey mixture; sauté lightly, stirring constantly. Add remaining ingredients; blend well. Cover and steam briefly. Season with pepper.

- **Tomato Pimiento Andalusia**   Omit flour, paprika, curry powder, basil, and broth. Adjust pimiento measure and add ingredients as follows:

4 ounces Neufchatel cheese, softened
⅓ to ½ cup Italian-style tomatoes,
    peeled and chopped
¼ cup chopped pimiento

¼ cup minced scallions
1 teaspoon dried whole oregano leaves
    Cayenne pepper to taste

Mix all ingredients into turkey mixture.

Veal Ragout

Makes 4 servings

2 pounds veal stew meat, cut in 1½-inch cubes
  Juice of 2 lemons
2 tablespoons vegetable oil
1 large carrot, peeled and sliced
1 rib celery, sliced
1 onion, studded with 1 whole clove
1½ cups Chicken Broth (recipe on page 121)
1 cup dry white wine

1 bouquet garni (parsley sprig, ½ bay leaf,
  4 peppercorns)
1 package (10 ounces) frozen baby pearl
  onions
½ pound small mushrooms, trimmed
4 ounces Neufchatel cheese
  Minced parsley

In a Dutch oven, combine veal, half of lemon juice, and water to cover. Bring to a boil; reduce heat. Simmer 2 to 3 minutes or until scum ceases to rise to surface. Drain veal, rinse, and wipe out kettle. Heat oil in kettle. Brown veal over high heat. Cook for 2 minutes. Add carrot, celery, whole onion, broth, wine, and bouquet garni. Bring to a boil; reduce heat. Simmer, covered, for 1½ hours or until veal is tender. Add onions and cook 10 minutes. Add mushrooms and cook 10 minutes. Remove veal and vegetables with a slotted spoon. Discard bouquet garni. Reduce liquid over high heat to about 1½ cups. Blend in remaining lemon juice and cheese. Return veal and vegetables to sauce. Stir to blend. Transfer to a serving dish. Sprinkle with parsley and serve.

Soupe au Pistou

Makes 6 servings

¾ cup dried red kidney beans
2 cups diced red onions
3 large boiling potatoes, peeled and diced
4 tomatoes, peeled, seeded, and chopped
¾ pound green beans, trimmed and cut
  into 1-inch pieces
2 zucchini squash, cubed
2 crookneck squash, cubed

1 cup whole wheat or spinach spaghetti,
  broken up
¼ teaspoon freshly ground pepper
  Pinch saffron powder
½ cup firmly packed basil leaves
4 cloves garlic
¼ cup grated Parmesan or Sapsago cheese

The night before cooking, rinse and sort beans. Place beans and water to cover in a 6-quart kettle. Soak overnight. Cover and bring to a boil. Reduce heat and simmer 45 minutes or until beans are tender. Drain well. Fill a 4-quart saucepan half full with water. Add onions and potatoes. Simmer for 40 minutes. Add tomatoes, kidney beans, green beans, zucchini and crookneck squash, spaghetti, pepper, and saffron; simmer for 15 minutes. Just before serving, pound the basil, garlic, and cheese together in a mortar until a smooth paste forms. Stir paste into soup and serve.

NUTRITIONAL INFORMATION PER SERVING

Calories	259	Saturated Fat	0.6g	Fiber	4.16g	Potassium	1390mg
Protein	12.5g	Cholesterol	4mg	Calcium	232mg	Sodium	81mg
Total Fat	2.1g	Carbohydrates	57.4g	Iron	4.4mg		

Navarin of Lamb
Makes 4 servings

2 pounds lamb shoulder, cut in 1½-inch cubes
  Salt and freshly ground pepper
1 tablespoon safflower oil
4 cups Chicken Broth (recipe on page 121)
1 to 2 cloves garlic, minced or pressed
1 bay leaf, broken in half
¼ teaspoon thyme or rosemary leaves
2 large tomatoes, seeded and chopped

4 new potatoes, quartered
4 turnips, peeled, quartered, and cut
  in 1½-inch pieces
4 carrots, peeled, quartered, and cut
  in 1½-inch pieces
1 package (10 ounces) frozen pearl onions
1 package (10 ounces) frozen early peas,
  thawed

Season lamb with salt and pepper. In a large saucepan or Dutch oven, heat oil. Brown meat on all sides. Remove lamb from pan; pat dry with paper towels. Wipe pan clean. Return meat to pan. Add broth, garlic, bay leaf, thyme, and tomatoes. Bring to a boil; reduce heat. Simmer about 1½ hours or until lamb is tender. After 45 minutes, add potatoes, turnips, and carrots. Simmer 20 minutes. Add onions; cook about 20 more minutes. Add peas in the last 5 minutes of cooking time. Remove meat and vegetables from pan. Skim fat from the cooking liquid. Return lamb to pan. Gently stir lamb and vegetables together. Adjust seasonings. Heat through and serve.

NUTRITIONAL INFORMATION PER SERVING

Calories	485	Saturated Fat	4.7g	Fiber	4.92g	Potassium	1565mg
Protein	51.8g	Cholesterol	93mg	Calcium	149mg	Sodium	592mg
Total Fat	15.0g	Carbohydrates	49.6g	Iron	7.2mg		

One-Pot Goulash
Makes 8 servings

2 pounds beef round, fat trimmed, cut in cubes
1 tablespoon safflower oil
1½ cups water
2 red onions, chopped
½ teaspoon salt
¼ teaspooon freshly ground pepper

1 tablespoon paprika
½ teaspoon caraway seeds
1 can (8 ounces) tomatoes
1 can (8 ounces) tomato puree
8 ounces fusili noodles, multi-colored and
  fresh, if possible

In a heavy Dutch oven or pressure cooker, brown meat in oil. Add water and heat to boiling. Drain off water into separate container; set aside to allow fat to rise to surface. Skim off fat with a bulb-type baster; then return liquid to pot. Stir in all remaining ingredients except noodles. Cover and simmer over very low heat until tender, 1 hour or more, or, cook in a pressure cooker for 20 minutes, following manufacturer's directions. Stir in uncooked noodles. Cover and cook an additional 10 to 12 minutes (or 5 minutes under pressure). Add more water, if needed.

NUTRITIONAL INFORMATION PER SERVING

Calories	220	Saturated Fat	0.8g	Fiber	0.67g	Potassium	523mg
Protein	24.7g	Cholesterol	8mg	Calcium	30mg	Sodium	350mg
Total Fat	3.7g	Carbohydrates	21.0g	Iron	4.0mg		

Navarin of Lamb, this page

Hearty Bean Soup

Makes 12 servings

1 pound (2½ cups) dried black beans
1 tablespoon safflower or olive oil
1 large red or yellow onion, chopped
2 carrots, peeled and shredded
2 ribs celery, sliced
3 to 5 cloves garlic, minced
1½ quarts Vegetable or Chicken Broth
   (recipes on pages 114 and 121)

4 tomatoes, diced
2 cups cooked brown rice
1 bay leaf
1½ teaspoons ground cumin
1 teaspoon oregano leaves
1 teaspoon salt
3 tablespoons red wine vinegar
Sliced radishes or lemon wedges, optional

The night before cooking, rinse and sort beans. Place beans and water to cover in a 4- or 5-quart kettle. Soak overnight. Cover and bring to a boil; reduce heat. Simmer 30 to 45 minutes or until most of the water is absorbed. While beans are cooking, heat oil in a 4-quart saucepan over medium heat. Add onion, carrots, celery, and garlic. Sauté, stirring often, until onion is tender. Add broth, tomatoes, rice, seasonings, and vinegar; simmer 15 minutes. In a blender or food processor, blend about 2 cups of the beans and ½ cup soup until smooth. Return to saucepan. Heat until steaming. Serve garnished with sliced radishes or lemon wedges, if desired.

NUTRITIONAL INFORMATION PER SERVING

Calories 222	Saturated Fat 0.2g	Fiber 2.38g	Potassium 682mg
Protein 12.5g	Cholesterol 0mg	Calcium 89mg	Sodium 211mg
Total Fat 2.2g	Carbohydrates 42.1g	Iron 3.6mg	

Chicken Cacciatore

Makes 4 servings

1 frying chicken (3 pounds), cut up and skinned
¼ cup all-purpose flour
1 tablespoon safflower oil
1 red onion, chopped
2 to 3 cloves garlic, minced
3 cups whole tomatoes, chopped

1 cup tomato paste
½ cup dry white wine
1 bay leaf
¼ teaspoon each pepper, thyme and marjoram

Dredge chicken in flour. In a skillet, sauté chicken in oil until golden brown. Add onion and garlic; brown lightly. In a blender or food processor, blend remaining ingredients. Stir into chicken mixture. Simmer, uncovered, until chicken is tender, about 45 minutes, adding water if needed. Serve with noodles.

NUTRITIONAL INFORMATION PER SERVING

Calories 404	Saturated Fat 2.5g	Fiber 1.51g	Potassium 1419mg
Protein 37.6g	Cholesterol 98mg	Calcium 75mg	Sodium 131mg
Total Fat 12.2g	Carbohydrates 37.2g	Iron 5.3mg	

Chicken or Beef Broth

Makes about 3 quarts (12 servings)

12 to 14 pounds chicken or beef bones and
   scraps (cooked, raw, or combination)
   (If making beef broth, make up total weight
   using ⅓ bones and ⅔ scraps.)
5 medium red onions, cut in chunks
5 medium carrots, peeled and cut in chunks
1 medium turnip, cut in chunks
1 rib celery, cut in chunks

8 to 10 parsley sprigs
8 to 10 black peppercorns
¼ cup peeled and sliced ginger root
¼ cup lemon juice
2 bay leaves
1 teaspoon thyme leaves
5 quarts water

Spread meat and bones on a large rimmed baking sheet. Bake at 400° F. for 1 hour 15 minutes. Transfer bones, scraps, and drippings to a 10-quart kettle. Rinse baking sheet with water, scraping browned bits from the bottom of the pan into the kettle. Add remaining ingredients. Bring to a boil; reduce heat. Cover and simmer for 4 hours. Cool slightly and discard large bones. Strain broth through a large colander. To remove sediment, strain again through colander lined with cheesecloth. Chill broth. Discard fat. Do not add salt so that if broth is reduced later it will not become too salty. Can be refrigerated up to 1 week or frozen.

NUTRITIONAL INFORMATION PER SERVING (Beef Broth)

Calories 16	Saturated Fat 0.2g	Fiber 0.00g	Potassium 130mg
Protein 2.7g	Cholesterol 0mg	Calcium 15mg	Sodium 32mg
Total Fat 0.5g	Carbohydrates 0.1g	Iron 0.4mg	

NUTRITIONAL INFORMATION PER SERVING (Chicken Broth)

Calories 39	Saturated Fat 0.4g	Fiber 0.00g	Potassium 210mg
Protein 4.9g	Cholesterol 1mg	Calcium 9mg	Sodium 78mg
Total Fat 1.3g	Carbohydrates 0.9g	Iron 0.5mg	

DESSERTS

Fruit Sorbet

Makes 1 quart (4 servings)

Colorful fruit sorbets or ices are lovely as desserts or as refreshments between courses. Try them as toppings for melons, or serve in fluted lemon or orange shells.

**4 cups strawberries and raspberries
or chopped peaches and nectarines**

**½ cup orange juice
Fructose or sugar to taste**

In a blender or food processor, puree berries or peaches and nectarines. If using berries, you may want to strain through a sieve to remove seeds. Add orange juice and fructose to taste; blend well. Pour into a shallow freezer pan; freeze until solid. Remove from freezer; let stand at room temperature until just soft enough to break up with a spoon. Beat with an electric mixer on low speed until fairly smooth, then beat on high speed until very smooth. Can be kept frozen in a tightly covered container for up to 2 months.

NUTRITIONAL INFORMATION PER SERVING

Calories 97	Saturated Fat 0.0g	Fiber 2.2g	Potassium 279mg
Protein 1.2g	Cholesterol 0mg	Calcium 27.5mg	Sodium 1.2mg
Total Fat 0.6g	Carbohydrates 23.0g	Iron 0.7mg	

Fruit Sorbet, this page; Floating Islands, 124

Floating Islands
Makes 4 servings
Show off this spectacular dessert with its contrasting berry sauce.

1½ teaspoons cream of tartar
5 egg whites
3 to 4 tablespoons fructose or sugar

1 cup Berry Sauce
Thin slices chilled mango, kiwi fruit, or tiny fresh mint leaves, optional

In a 3- or 4-quart saucepan, bring 2 quarts water and cream of tartar to a boil. Reduce heat; keep water simmering. In a large mixing bowl, beat egg whites until soft peaks form. Slowly add fructose, beating until stiff peaks form. With a spatula, mound ¼ of the whites onto a perforated skimmer and smooth gently into a dome-shaped "island." Gently place skimmer on the surface of the water until egg white is released and floats on the water. Rinse and dry the skimmer. Repeat for 3 more islands. Simmer 6 to 7 minutes; turn and simmer 6 to 7 minutes or until egg whites are set. Drain on a clean towel; cool. To serve, chill 4 dessert plates. Spread the Berry Sauce in the centers of the plates and place an island in the center of each. Garnish with fruit and mint, if desired.

Berry Sauce

¼ cup fructose or sugar
¼ cup water
½ pound fresh strawberries, raspberries, or blackberries or 1 package (10 ounces) thawed frozen berries

1 to 2 tablespoons lemon juice to taste or Kirsch or Cassis to taste, optional

In a bowl, dissolve fructose in water. In a blender or food processor, puree berries and sugar-water. Strain sauce through a sieve, pressing the berries through with a spoon. Stir in lemon juice and kirsch, if desired. Store in a covered container in the refrigerator.

NUTRITIONAL INFORMATION PER SERVING

Calories ... 157	Saturated Fat ... 0.0g	Fiber ... 0.61g	Potassium ... 144mg
Protein ... 4.4g	Cholesterol ... 0mg	Calcium ... 13mg	Sodium ... 64mg
Total Fat ... 0.1g	Carbohydrates ... 32.1g	Iron ... 0.1mg	

Bananas with Moscovite Apricot Sauce

Makes 4 servings

¼ cup water
1 to 2 tablespoons fructose or sugar
½ cup Moscovite Apricot Sauce
Scant ¼ teaspoon almond extract

1 teaspoon vanilla
4 ripe bananas, peeled
Mint sprigs, optional

Preheat oven to 425° F. In a saucepan, bring water to a boil. Stir in fructose; remove from heat. Add apricot sauce and almond extract; blend well with a wire whisk. To make boat-shaped containers, fold four 12-inch-long sheets of aluminum foil lengthwise in half. Fold ends in and pinch corners together. Place a banana in each foil boat. Pour 3 tablespoons of the apricot sauce over each banana. Sprinkle almond extract and vanilla over each. Fold top edges of foil over and pinch together securely. Place boats on a large baking sheet. Bake for 20 minutes. Place boats on heated serving plates, open foil, and garnish with mint sprigs before serving, if desired.

Moscovite Apricot Sauce

*Delicious served over hot fruit compotes, frozen yogurt, pound cake,
or anything you can dream up.*

12 ripe apricots, rinsed, halved, and pitted or
1 can (16 ounces) unsweetened apricot halves, drained and rinsed
½ cup water (only if using fresh apricots)

1 vanilla bean or ½ teaspoon vanilla
2 tablespoons fructose or sugar
1 to 2 teaspoons lemon juice

In a saucepan, combine all ingredients. Bring to a boil; reduce heat. Simmer for 10 to 15 minutes or until mixture is reduced by about one-third and is moderately thick. Remove vanilla bean. Puree apricots in a blender or food processor. Store in a tightly covered container in the refrigerator.

NUTRITIONAL INFORMATION PER SERVING

Calories	230	Saturated Fat	0.0g	Fiber	1.6g	Potassium	835mg
Protein	3.1g	Cholesterol	0mg	Calcium	29mg	Sodium	2mg
Total Fat	0.7g	Carbohydrates	56.7g	Iron	0.14mg		

Ginger Frosted Fruit

Makes 4 servings

The buzz words "quick and easy" come to mind with this dessert.

½ cup sour half-and-half or kefir
1 tablespoon honey
1 tablespoon chopped candied ginger
1 lemon

1 Red Delicious apple
1 Granny Smith apple
1 kiwi fruit, peeled and sliced
3 bananas, diagonally sliced

Make a dip by combining sour half-and-half, honey, and candied ginger; set aside. Cut lemon in half. Cut one half in slices; squeeze juice from remaining half. Slice apples. Arrange fruit on a serving platter. Garnish with lemon slices. Sprinkle lemon juice over banana and apple slices. Cover with plastic wrap until ready to serve. Serve with sour half-and-half dip.

NUTRITIONAL INFORMATION PER SERVING

Calories 199	Saturated Fat 1.4g	Fiber 1.39g	Potassium 535mg
Protein 4.6g	Cholesterol 9mg	Calcium 99mg	Sodium 76mg
Total Fat 2.7g	Carbohydrates 43.4g	Iron 1.0mg	

Lemon Orange Thins

Makes about 60

A snappy, piquant cookie that will enhance a multitude of desserts.

1½ cups flour
½ teaspoon baking soda
¼ teaspoon salt
¼ cup vegetable shortening
¼ cup butter

¾ cup packed brown sugar
1 egg
1 tablespoon lemon juice
2 teaspoons grated lemon peel
1 to 2 teaspoons grated orange peel

In a bowl, stir together flour, baking soda, and salt; set aside. In a mixing bowl, cream the shortening, butter, and brown sugar until smooth. Blend in egg. Add lemon juice and fruit peel; blend well. Stir in dry ingredients. Shape dough into two 6-inch rolls. Wrap tightly with waxed paper or plastic wrap. Chill overnight. Preheat oven to 375° F. Cut dough into slices a little over ⅛ inch thick. Place cookies about 1 inch apart on an ungreased baking sheet. Bake for 8 to 10 minutes or until edges are golden. Remove from baking sheet to a wire rack to cool.

NUTRITIONAL INFORMATION PER SERVING (5 cookies)

Calories 192	Saturated Fat 3.6g	Fiber 0.03g	Potassium 78mg
Protein 2.3g	Cholesterol 33mg	Calcium 19mg	Sodium 103mg
Total Fat 8.7g	Carbohydrates 26.6g	Iron 1.1mg	

Petite Pear Soufflés

Makes 5 servings

3 to 4 very ripe pears (about 1 pound)
1½ cups water
1½ cups sparkling cider
1 tablespoon brown sugar
¼ cup sugar or fructose

1 vanilla bean, split lengthwise
½ to 1 teaspoon Eau de Vie de Poire
  (pear liqueur) or kirsch
2 egg yolks, lightly beaten
6 egg whites

Peel, quarter, and core pears. In a saucepan, combine water, cider, sugars, and vanilla bean. Bring to a boil. Add pears; simmer for 10 to 15 minutes or until tender; drain. In a blender or food processor, puree pears and liqueur. Transfer puree to a bowl. Add egg yolks; blend well. Preheat oven to 425° F. In a small bowl, beat egg whites until soft peaks form. Fold about one-third of the egg whites into the puree with a small whisk. Gently fold in remaining egg whites with a rubber spatula. Spoon soufflé batter into ungreased individual molds or custard cups. With a spatula, make a ½-inch-deep groove ½ inch from edge of each mold. Reduce oven temperature to 375° F. Bake soufflés for 8 to 10 minutes or until puffy and golden. Serve at once.

NUTRITIONAL INFORMATION PER SERVING

Calories 215	Saturated Fat 0.7g	Fiber 1.99g	Potassium 322mg
Protein 5.6g	Cholesterol 109mg	Calcium 36mg	Sodium 67mg
Total Fat 2.8g	Carbohydrates 43.0g	Iron 1.0mg	

Creme Amandine

Makes 4 servings

2 eggs, lightly beaten
1½ cups skim milk, scalded
2 tablespoons sugar
¼ teaspoon vanilla

¼ teaspoon almond extract
Boiling water
Allspice
Sliced almonds, toasted

In a bowl, combine eggs, milk, sugar, vanilla, and almond extract; blend well. Pour into four 6-ounce custard cups coated with nonstick vegetable spray. Place cups in a large skillet. Add boiling water to reach two-thirds up sides of cups. Heat until water is just below boiling; reduce heat. Do not boil or custard will curdle. Cover and simmer 12 minutes or until a knife inserted in the center comes out clean. Remove cups from water. Sprinkle with allspice and toasted almonds. Serve warm or cold.

NUTRITIONAL INFORMATION PER SERVING

Calories 110	Saturated Fat 1.0g	Fiber 0.11g	Potassium 204mg
Protein 6.5g	Cholesterol 139mg	Calcium 134mg	Sodium 82mg
Total Fat 4.1g	Carbohydrates 11.4g	Iron 0.7mg	

I·N·D·E·X